EVALUATING LOCAL ENVIRONMENTAL POLICY

Evaluating Local Environmental Policy

Edited by
STUART M. FARTHING
School of Town and Country Planning
Faculty of the Built Environment
University of the West of England, Bristol

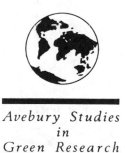

Avebury Studies
in
Green Research

Aldershot · Brookfield USA · Hong Kong · Singapore · Sydney

© S. M. Farthing 1997

Published by
Avebury
Ashgate Publishing Ltd
Gower House
Croft Road
Aldershot
Hants GU11 3HR
England

Ashgate Publishing Company
Old Post Road
Brookfield
Vermont 05036
USA

British Library Cataloguing in Publication Data

Farthing, Stuart M.
    Evaluating local environmental policy. - (Avebury studies
    in green research)
    1. Environmental policy - Great Britain 2. Environmental
    protection - Great Britain 3. Land use - Great Britain -
    Planning
    I. Title
    333.7 ' 3 ' 0941

    ISBN 1 85972 321 7

Library of Congress Catalog Card Number: 96-78546

Printed and bound by Athenaeum Press, Ltd.,
Gateshead, Tyne & Wear.

Contents

Figures, tables and photographs

FIGURES

PHOTOGRAPHS

List of contributors

John Baker is a consultant with Baker Associates and Associate Lecturer at UWE, Bristol. He has conducted research on the environmental appraisal of development plans.

Hugh Barton is Senior Lecturer in Town & Country Planning at UWE, Bristol. He has published in the fields of public transport, environmental planning and environmental assessment, including recently a book for Earthscan on local Environmental Auditing (with Noel Bruder), and Sustainable Settlements guide for planners, designers and developers (with Richard Guise). He is currently researching urban eco-villages.

Noel Bruder is a national campaigns co-ordinator with Earth Watch/Friends of the Earth Ireland. He is currently working on a number of projects which aim to highlight the importance of sustainable development in an Irish context.

Tessa Coombes is a Researcher with the Severnside Planning and Environment Unit in the Faculty of the Built Environment at UWE, Bristol. She is also a local councillor in Bristol and is Chair of the Green Initiatives Joint Sub-Commitee. She is currently researching jobs in the sustainable economy and community involvement in Local Agenda 21.

Stuart Farthing is Principal Lecturer in Town & Country Planning at UWE, Bristol. He has published on a variety of topics including information technology in planning practice, landowner involvement in land use planning and most recently planning for affordable housing.

Martin Fodor is Environmental Coordinator at Bristol's CREATE Centre where he coordinates the council Eco Management and Audit scheme, the Green Charter Annual Action Plan and other initiatives. A graduate of St

Andrews University, he is the author of many articles on the subject of solar power, energy saving buildings and sustainable development.

Richard Guise is an architect and planner specialising in conservation and urban design at UWE, Bristol. He is co-author with Hugh Barton of the Design Guide for Sustainable Settlements published by LGMB and UWE in 1995. He is leader of the Traditional Paving Research Project at UWE.

Tony Harrison is Principal Lecturer in Town & Country Planning at UWE, Bristol. His research interests are land use planning systems and land policy. He has recently published *Attitudes to Town & Country* (with Peter McCarthy).

Geoff Mills is Principal Transport Policy Officer at North Somerset District Council. He formerly held posts at Avon County Council responsible for transport policy and for bus service planning.

Graham Pinfield is Head of Environmental Policy in the Planning Department of Lancashire County Council. He sat on the Steering Group of the LGMB National Sustainability Indicators project and is on the editorial board of Town and Country Planning magaazine.

Dominic Stead is Lecturer in Town & Country Planning at UWE, Bristol. His current reearch interests are planning and environmental issues, particularly the effects of land use planning on transport and the environment. He is also currently involved in contributing to a new book on greening the curriculum in further and higher education.

John Winter is Associate Dean in the Faculty of the Built Environment, UWE, Bristol. His research interests are the quality of the environments on new housing developments, and professional mobility in the EU. He has published on the effectiveness of statutory local plans, and the environmental quality and the sustainability of large scale private sector housing schemes.

1 Introduction

Stuart Farthing

In the field of environmental policy there is no doubt that there is great current interest in *local* environmental policy. Three changes appear to have led to this interest. First, there is a recognition that despite the significance of global environmental issues such as global warming, or ozone depletion, many environmental issues are local. This means that the benefits (and the costs) of environmental goods are available to a population in a restricted area but equally that some changes which threaten human health or well-being or the survival of natural eco-systems are also spatially restricted. Changes to the built environment of an area through economic development, the loss of valued open landscapes through new development, pollution of water courses through leachate from landfill tips are examples of how 'the environment' is seen as being threatened. Though, in practice, it may be difficult to draw the boundaries of impact and though some local damage may be 'exported', it is nevertheless likely that these impacts are spatially restricted.

A second change that has raised interest in local environmental policy is the recognition that how people live their daily lives *within localities* can have a significant impact on the environment. A key concern here is the transport sector which causes local environmental problems (noise, fumes, accidents and air pollution) threatening to local health and life but also emissions of CO_2 implicated in global warming. If the environment is to be protected and human health and quality of life maintained then, it is argued, there will have to be major even radical change in life styles. Whilst there is scope for debate about this, there is a recognition that local social processes, as opposed to national or international processes, help to produce and reproduce the routines of daily life.

The final change has been recognition that local *policy*, policy and practice at the level of local government, is an important determinant of environmental outcomes. This reflects not only the long standing concerns of local government with environmental regulation in, for example, noise or control of atmospheric pollution through smoke control but also a recognition that local government policies not traditionally seen as environmental have significant environmental impacts. Policies for the provision of facilities and services in residential areas and for the floorscape of the public realm, discussed in later chapters, are good examples. There is now therefore considerable discussion of the role of local government in environmental matters (Hams et al 1994; Stoker and Young 1993; Agyeman and Evans 1994). The Earth Summit at Rio concluded with a commitment from governments to prepare sustainable development plans and a commitment to local government involvement in that process. For local government in the UK, this represented a significant shift from the attitudes and centralising tendencies of the 1980s. For land use planning, a key policy area, the change has been dramatic: 'From its vulnerable and subservient position in the early 1980s, planning is now officially seen as a key instrument in delivering land use and development objectives that are compatible with the aim of sustainable development' (Selman 1995, 291). But there remains a wider debate about the power and resources of local government to tackle environmental problems.

The new role of local government is increasingly as an 'enabler' rather than a 'provider' of goods and services. In the context of environmental strategies, Hams et al (1994,15) suggest that: 'The local authority's role in developing and implementing such agreed local environmental strategies will, to a considerable extent, be as catalyst, convenor and coordinator rather than as executor; its educational, promotional and enabling functions will prove as important as its direct regulatory responsibilities.' Such an approach, however, can be seen to pose considerable risks to a local authority in terms of delivering satisfactory outcomes since success is dependent on the cooperation of a range of actors and organisations in the local area (Marshall 1994). In this situation it could be argued that a major lever that local government has to bring about change is a policy or strategy statement. There has thus been a renewed debate about the meaning of policy, and growing interest in the methodology of policy- and decision-making (see for example Wilson 1993) and in more 'rational' processes of research for policy (LARIA 1995). There has also been a growth in the publication of environmental charters, environmental audits, state of the environment reports and environmental action plans (Ward 1993)

However there is a recognition that the debate about local environmental policy needs to move on from the raising of the profile of environmental issues and sustainability to the evaluation of policy. This is not to deny the important battle still to be waged in some areas in legitimising environmental policy (Golding 1994) but it explains why work, for example, is being conducted into processes of environmental auditing, into the development of indicators of sustainability. In general, there seems to be a growing commitment amongst a number of researchers and policy-makers to exploring the role of evaluation in the improvement of environmental policy. In order to help promote such a development and with the aim of exploring these issues, a conference was held in 1994 at the University of the West of England, Bristol. The chapters which follow are updated and developed versions of the papers given at the conference with a

2

few that have been subsequently commissioned for the book.

Whilst there is no party line or single theme which dominates the book, all the contributors are committed to the belief that evaluation has a significant role to play in sharpening the debate about local environmental policy. But equally there is a view that in evaluating environmental policy some of the implicit views and assumptions connected with 'evaluation' and 'policy' have to be re-thought or at least questioned. This is not to suggest that environmental policy necessarily raises qualitatively new issues for research and evaluation. Indeed the main assumption of the book is that much of what is seen as distinctive about environmental policy - the complexity of the issues involved, the need for corporate working in local government, the active participation of the local community - are long standing concerns of local policy and implementation. However, there is scope for believing that engagement with the environmental debate raises questions about the assumptions of policy and questions which relate to some long-standing disputes in policy evaluation.

Assumptions of policy questioned by environmental issues

The environmental agenda and concern for sustainability has raised questions about some of the previously unexamined assumptions of much public policy. These are, by now, well-recognised in the academic and governmental literature but not necessarily in the policy process itself. A number of commentators have pointed to the challenge they provide to conventional local policy processes (eg Hams et al 1994; Hill and Smith 1994). Four of the most significant are the 'rights' of nature, the treatment of spatial and temporal issues, and the precautionary principle.

Traditionally policy has been concerned with the well-being of human populations and policy evaluations have been concerned with the degree to which policy brings about significant improvements to well-being. But the environmental movement, as mentioned earlier, has raised questions about the desirability of protecting the environment or nature not for the sake of human populations but for the sake of the natural environment itself. Deep green approaches place emphasis on the rights of nature but the definition of sustainability given by Brundtland - 'development that meets the needs of the present without compromising the ability of future generations to meet their own needs' (World Commission on Environment and Development 1987, 43) - seems to place the emphasis clearly on humanity and the continued (though sustainable) exploitation of natural resources.

In addition to the question of the impact of policy on nature and the environment, there is the question of the impact of policy over space. In evaluating social and economic policies governments have traditionally sought to assess benefits and costs to residents of their state or locality. Whilst it is recognised that there can be effects beyond the locality or the state, these have not been of prime concern and

3

have been ignored. For example, in the analytical work for the Third London Airport in the early 1970s, the question of the travel costs and benefits to foreign nationals having to travel to and from different proposed sites for the Third London Airport was raised but concluded in favour of ignoring such impacts. Although local environmental issues were hotly disputed in that debate, the wider, even global consequences of those travel patterns in term of the emissions of greenhouse gases were ignored. These points about the different spatial scales at which environmental impacts can be felt are familiar but they challenge some of the assumptions that underpinned previous national or local responses to problems and require some recognition in evaluation efforts. According to the LGMB (1994) some countries, including the Netherlands which uses the concept of 'eco-scope' are starting to assess their external impact.

There is the growing recognition of the importance, even centrality, of the impacts of policy over time. Traditionally policy has been concerned with the present or the immediate future. Politicians have been blamed for taking an exceptionally short-term electorally-based perspective on the costs and benefits of policies. Yet the thrust of sustainability is towards concern for future generations rather than the present. These raise questions about inter-generational equity, the interest of current generations in the well-being of future generations. This is at once a moral and an empirical question (Jacobs 1994). Traditional cost-benefit approaches tend to discount the future very highly whether the concern is future benefits or costs. There is also the question of prediction and the whole issue of uncertainty surrounding policy consequences. There are considerable problems predicting short-term let alone the longer term consequences of policies (Blowers 1993).

This raises the debate about the 'precautionary principle' which advocates that policies and decisions should take account of the uncertainty of environmental understanding and 'where there are threats of serious or irreversible damage, lack of full scientific certainty should not be used as a reason for postponing cost-effective measures to prevent environmental degradation' (UNCED, 1993, Principle 15). Whilst recognition of the possibility of damage to critical life support systems may crucially raise the stakes in policy, uncertainty about systems being managed and of the impact of policy measures has been a well-recognised feature of local policy and decision taking for some time (see, for example, Friend and Jessop 1977, Rosenhead 1989). Its rise to prominence in international debates about the environment arises from a mistaken belief in the possibility of certain scientific knowledge as the basis for policy. The message for analysis would seem to be, therefore, that evaluative efforts should be as open as possible about the uncertainties involved in any policy situation. One might add that uncertainties apply not just to uncertainties of impact of policy measures, but also to uncertainties about values and the objectives to be attained, or trade-offs to be accepted between different environmental goods (see in particular Chapter 8), and also uncertainties introduced by the impact of decision-making in related areas.

4

Debates in policy evaluation

Whilst it is possible to overstate the consensus and agreement between policy-makers on the issues discussed above, it is true that there are many areas where there is disagreement and debate amongst policy analysts about policy evaluation. Here new attempts to integrate environmental policy objectives with social and economic policies provide a new opportunity to reflect on those debates. Particular attention is given here to the debate about the utilisation of evaluation, the users of evaluation, the role of experts in evaluation and the methodology of evaluation.

Utilisation

A fundamental question in policy evaluation is how the success of an evaluation, as an evaluation, is to be measured. Most commentators suggest that an evaluation should be utilised but the way it is utilised and by whom is the subject of considerable debate. On the one hand, there is the view that the success of policy evaluation is to be measured by the extent to which there is direct, immediate impact on practice. On the other hand, some analysts seem to take the view that utilisation is more of a conceptual activity, and evaluation is a contribution to the debate about policy. One way of characterising this debate is to see it as a dispute between what have been called the 'engineering' and 'enlightenment' models of research (Janowitz 1972). The 'engineering' model is adopted by those who expect environmental policy to be strongly shaped by research, who see evaluative studies therefore as playing a strong role in shaping future policy measures. Those who subscribe to the 'enlightenment' model take the view that research, such as the outputs of processes of environmental auditing and other evaluative studies, is only one influence on the policy process and not a very significant one at that - the forces that drive policy change are interests. Groups bargain and negotiate on the basis of their interests in order to shape and direct policy and practice. Indeed the distinction between policy and practice breaks down. Practice, the routine interactions between actors, becomes policy. Evaluation and research give actors a language and a set of concepts that they can use to understand the environmental problem. Research may be used politically to argue for a particular approach. It thus has a more diffuse and long term impact on the policy agenda than the engineering model suggests.

Users of evaluation

These differences in conceptualisation of use are also reflected in the type of user or the perceived audience for evaluation. An emphasis on utilisation as direct impact on practice tends to focus attention on practitioners and a relatively small group of pre-identified users or stakeholders as users of policy evaluation. But an emphasis on the conceptual or theoretical contribution of policy evaluation suggests a wider, more diffuse group of users, less easily identifiable than practitioners. It seems likely that many early efforts at environmental evaluation in local government (for example environmental auditing discussed in Chapter 2) had a very unclear view about who exactly the users or audience were intended to be. And this may well account for some of the difficulty experienced with the process.

The question of the audience for evaluation captures an important dilemma for those seeking to evaluate environmental policy. It is widely perceived that environmental quality and outcomes are linked quite directly to the way people live within localities and that significant, even radical, change in life styles may be needed to bring about a more sustainable society. Policy evaluation thus should be directed at the local community, at changing their perceptions and understandings of environmental issues so that they may accept, or even demand, changes in policy. This is undoubtedly the viewpoint behind much work on indicators of sustainability, discussed in Chapter 4. Yet, if changing public understanding is the target, it may be difficult to point to clear success in this respect and the work that has been done may not feed very satisfactorily into change in behaviour of the implementers of local environmental policy *within* local government.

However, evaluative activities that seek to make significant change to local practice, to influence practitioners in different areas of local government activity, such as the work on the environmental appraisal of development plans discussed in Chapter 3, may be faced with the recognition that whatever the local authority does, it does not in any meaningful sense control the field of activity in a direct way (it has few powers and resources) and therefore depends crucially on others to take action to implement policies. Indeed, the insertion of concepts, such as environmental capacity discussed in Chapter 6, into local policy debate may generate competing definitions of capacity from other policy actors. The success of such evaluative work may therefore be just as difficult to identify.

The role of experts in evaluation

A related question concerns the role of experts in evaluation. Is the role to help the users or potential users ('the clients') to define their *own* questions for evaluation or to help clients define *relevant* or important questions at stake in the issue? This has clear relevance for the environmental debate. A strong theme in environmental discussion is the view that experts, scientists and, to a lesser extent, social scientists, can provide authoritative guidance to policy makers and practitioners, defining key issues and identifying appropriate policy responses. The power of experts to influence the environmental agenda has been clear in the case of global warming and ozone depletion. Thus the role of experts according to this view is to raise the level of environmental knowledge and awareness. But the desire to accommodate to political realities, to the context of decision-making, may lead to a focus on questions that reflect the priorities and understandings of practitioners, or in the context of local environmental issues, the public.

This tension is reflected in the definition of sustainable development. 'Sustainable development is not just another name for environmental protection. It is concerned

6

with issues which are long term and effects which are irreversible. A new approach to policy making is required which does not trade-off short term costs and benefits but regards some aspects of the environment as absolute constraints.' (UK Local Government Declaration on Sustainable Development 1993). Here clearly whatever practitioners engaged in policy making and implementation or the wider public may feel about a topic, the implication is that expert opinion has to define long term issues and effects which are irreversible. The Local Government Management Board (1994) illustrates the tension in its discussion of the involvement of the public in the development of sustainable indicators. It advocates the active involvement of the public in sustainable development and its commitment to the development of indicators that are meaningful at the local level: 'a feeling of ownership is imperative for long term success' (LGMB 1994,27). However it also acknowledges the need to broaden understanding: 'community perceptions of the quality of life may need to be broadened to encompass, for example, their "footprint" on neighbouring communities'(LGMB 1994,27).

The LGMB view of indicators seems to be a technocratic one in which the problem of sustainable development can be defined by experts. Pragmatically, involvement of the public is important to test whether proposals are politically feasible or to educate the public about the issues. Other environmental commentators, however, point out the limit of expert knowledge of the environment. Blowers (1993) in a recent paper remarks on the strength of scientific consensus on ozone depletion and global warming but stresses that scientific evidence is often 'incomplete, provisional or uncertain' (Blowers 1993,781) and he goes on to suggest that science cannot provide definitive answers to environmental questions. Rather than providing a secure body of knowledge science may be better seen as a process of inquiry which raises questions and which tries to answer them through the interpretation of evidence and its significance. Others who might support the role of the evaluator as one which helps clients to define their own environmental questions stress the importance of values to the definition of problems (Jacobs 1993). Values influence the weight to be attached to different aspects of environmental problems (Hope and Parker 1995) and the selection of environmental problems themselves (Pearce et al 1991). The much discussed Seattle approach appears to exemplify this approach where there was widespread involvement of local people in deriving the indicators to be used and published (Biddick, 1995).

Methodology

There are also important debates within evaluation about the significance of the methodology adopted by evaluators. Rossi and Freeman (1989) suggest that there are two postures in relation to this debate - a purist scientific one and a pragmatic one. The scientific view is associated with Campbell (see Cook and Campbell 1979) who advocates the logic of the scientific method in the evaluation of policies and in particular the experiment. On the other side of the debate is Cronbach

(1982) who emphasises the need to be pragmatic and to recognise that each evaluation effort takes place in a particular social and political context and that the methodology needs to be adapted to the needs of the stakeholders and to the particular purposes of the evaluation. Patton (1986) similarly talks of the importance of 'utilization-focused' evaluation, the essence of which is that, first, the intended evaluation users must be identified and organised and, second, that evaluators must work with these specific stakeholders to make all other decisions about the evaluation including its methodology. Thus the focus, design, methods, analysis, interpretation and dissemination are decided collaboratively.

A parallel debate can be detected in relation to environmental policy in this respect. Despite his caveats about the current certainty of scientific understanding of environmental threats, Blowers (1993,784) seems to have faith that further interdisciplinary research across the natural sciences and between the natural and social sciences will lead to a greater consensus on the action that needs to be taken. A quite different perspective however can be seen in the work of Carley and Christie (1992). They advocate the use of *action research* derived from Schon (1983) in the management of sustainable development. They criticise the value of the traditional social scientific approach, modelled as it is on the natural sciences. It cannot cope with the dynamics of a policy situation characterised by turbulence, it means that 'qualitative aspects of environmental problems will be ignored or undervalued' (Carley and Christie 1992, 181-182). By contrast action research:

1   makes use of the social context of a specific environmental problem or development challenge to increase its own effects;
2   redefines the research process towards a rapid, interactive cycle of problem-discovery-reflection-response-problem redefinition;
3   replaces the neutral social scientist/observer with a multi-disciplinary team of practitioners and researchers, all working together in a process of mutual education;
4   proposes that pluralistic evaluation replace static models of social processes. This is characterised by concern for: institutional functioning, continual monitoring of project implementation, the subjective views of major constituent groups, and methodological 'triangulation' by which a variety of data sources are brought to bear for evaluation; and
5   generates replicable learning from the above elements, which is constantly tested against both past experience and the results of current action.

It is clear from this that the debate about methodology is very much on the agenda of those concerned with evaluating environmental policy. There are also grounds for suggesting that the environmental policy debate has neglected some important questions about evaluation which are as challenging to practice as some of the more conventional policy concerns expressed in the literature: about the compexity of environmental issues, importance of public involvement and intersectoral working.

Policy evaluation and the sharpening of environmental policy

The debate in much of the literature dealing with local environmental policy has tended to put the emphasis on the need to raise the profile of environmental issues in local government and to respond to the demands of Local Agenda 21. Hams et al (1994) suggest that local government has moved through two phases of environmental policy and is moving towards a third. The transition between phases is uneven, with certain authorities playing a leading role in changed policy and practice. In the first phase prior to about 1988, environmental policy was fragmented and largely unacknowledged. This is not to deny that environmental or local quality of life issues were important to local actors and activists. Planning authorities in the 'south' during the building and development boom of the 1980s faced opposition from local residents and local residents groups campaigning against 'growth' and further development. Arguments used covered both the negative impacts on the local environment and on the lack of facilities of various kinds to support the growing population. Evidence from research I have carried out in growth areas of Hampshire outside Southampton sheds some light on this issue. (Coombes, Farthing, and Winter 1990). There long standing local residents of 'growth sectors' - areas undergoing rapid urbanisation - complained about the decline in environmental quality: growing noise, pollution, dust, loss of open space and access to the countryside. In much of this environmental deterioration the car was implicated directly.

In the second phase of environmental policy for local government, the notion of sustainable development assumes a higher profile. Hams et al (1994) describe this phase as one in which environmental policy is conceived of in a more holistic way. First some policy areas have increased emphasis, for example, Nature Conservation Strategies, recycling, waste management and regulation. Then there have been attempts, in innovative local authorities, to create more coherent and integrated consideration of environmental issues through the appointment of environmental coordinators, the production of Green Charters and early attempts at the development of environmental management and audit systems to evaluate the environmental impacts of local authority activities. In the third phase of development, local authorities will it is hoped be informed by post-Rio commitments to sustainable development (Agenda 21). Local authorities have been presented with a mandate and the challenge to produce a Local Agenda 21 for their locality by 1996 and according to recent research quoted in Whittaker (1995) over half of local authorities have committed themselves to this objective but there remains some lack of will and a problem of resources in others (Rees and Wehrmeyer 1995).

Increasingly, there are debates and discussions about the processes of policy evaluation. There has, to take a particularly high profile concern, been a recent interest in the development of indicators and the setting of targets for measuring progress towards sustainability (LGMB 1994). The view taken here is, first, that evaluation is not concerned just with the assessment of policies after policy formulation and implementation, a view of evaluation that ignores the importance of evaluative issues at all stages in the policy process and ignores in particular the importance attached to the process by which policies are generated. Second, it is important to recognise as previous discussion above showed, that evaluation is inherently a political activity (Palumbo 1987).

What is striking is that much discussion in the literature on environmental policy fails to acknowledge the role of politics in this process. Whilst there are discussions of the need for 'partnership', for the active support and cooperation of all sectors of the local community, the importance of interests in defining and representing the environment and in evaluating environmental policy is not really developed. Perhaps in the literature of organisations like the Local Government Management Board, it is desirable to downplay the difficulties and emphasise consensus. Yet conflict is inevitable in the process of Local Agenda 21 as writers like Webber (1994) acknowledge.

The chapters which follow are all concerned in one way or another to develop a more critical, reflective and evaluative approach to local environmental policy and sustainability. A framework which helps to make sense of the place of evaluation within the policy process is through the notion of the 'policy cycle' (Nakamura and Smallwood 1980, Rist 1995). This cycle helps to identify the type of information and therefore type of policy evaluation which is required but it has to be recognised that this is an idealisation of the cycle. The first stage of the policy cycle is *agenda setting* (the terms here are taken from Palumbo 1987), when the question is whether the environment or sustainability are to be the subject of governmental action. This stage has clearly been passed with local environmental policy. The next step is *problem definition* which is crucial in terms of setting parameters to the subsequent design and implementation of policy. *Policy design* is concerned with the formulation of policies and the selection of the options which will most cost effectively address the problem as defined and these are then the subject of legitimation by politicians in the light of evidence of public support for the policy. Policies are then subject to *implementation*, and subsequently to assessments of impact. The final stage of the policy cycle is that of *termination*, when the policy may be modified or abandoned.

A number of commentators, and in particular the authors of Chapters 2 to 6 take the perspective that a more structured, formal approach to the environmental policy process is needed than the one that has hitherto existed and that within a more structured approach more formal methods and techniques of analysis can have some purchase on the policy design stage (environmental audits, sustainability indicators, targets, environmental capacity techniques). Whilst some might detect moves here back towards the rational approach to policy formulation evident in the 1960s and early 1970s, the emphasis in these chapters is on an approach which recognises that the context of policy-making for sustainable development is complex, uncertain and conflict-ridden.

Noel Bruder in Chapter 2 explores 'environmental auditing' by local authorities which is a process which has helped agenda setting and more particularly problem definition in local government. Environmental audits have both sought to describe the current state of the local environment and the impact on it of the policies and practices of the local authority. This shows that the notion of the policy cycle is a simplification of the actual process in local government, that the process can be defined in various ways and that there can be overlap between stages with assessments of impact feeding into early stages of the environmental policy process. However, Bruder argues that though environmental auditing has provided environmental information and some analysis, it has failed to engage with the political processes of policy design and implementation and in many (perhaps most) local authorities environmental policy has not progressed beyond this starting point. He therefore argues for a more 'strategic' view of the process of environmental auditing which both seeks an increased role for environmental evaluation in the policy cycle and recognises that for such activity to bear fruit in terms of more effective environmental policies then those analysts need to engage in political action within the local authority to change policy processes and institutional arrangements.

One area where the consideration of environmental issues and sustainable development has been forced onto the local authority agenda and more importantly into 'policy design' is in the production of development plans under the 1990 Town and Country Planning Act. John Baker in Chapter 3 looks at the recent policy advice and practice for the environmental appraisal of development plans involving as the Guidelines (DoE 1993) state 'an explicit, systematic and iterative review of development plan policies and proposals to evaluate their combined impacts on the environment'. Baker as part of the research team which drew up the guidelines accepts that evaluative concerns and values enter the policy process at all stages, and he rejects the notion that environmental appraisal of development plans is something which is merely undertaken at the end of the policy formulation process. Environmental concerns have to be built into the process and considered at the stage of defining the overall strategy of the development plan.

Acknowledgement of the potential for conflict and disagreement over environmental policy is clear in the chapter by Baker as it is in Bruder's chapter. Both, however, show that involving different groups in the environmental policy appraisal or audit process can have benefits in building legitimacy for decisions and recommendations both in terms of promoting consensus and giving credibility to the analysis of environmental problems. Both contributors, too, emphasise the importance of recognising that in addressing environmental issues we are dealing with problems on which our knowledge is in many cases uncertain. In attempting to bring environmental concerns into the decision-making calculus, predictions of the impact of policy measures on environmental stocks or components may lack any theoretical or empirical base. Judgement has a role to play here but so does research.

Perhaps the most important common ground between the two writers is the notion that environmental auditing and environmental appraisal should not just be seen as providing a set of tools or techniques so much as processes that can help to promote changed thinking and action on the environment.

Indicators of, and targets for, sustainability as well as the issue of environmental capacity discussed respectively in Chapters 4 to 6 can be seen as providing evaluative tools relevant at all stages of the policy cycle. They can help in agenda setting when they help to raise public concerns about the issues and raise pressure for action. They can help in assessing the scale of problems, in policy design and in assessing the impact of policies. This is one reason why they are currently generating so much interest in the debate about sustainability.

Graham Pinfield in Chapter 4 looks at the need and justification for sustainability indicators arising out of Agenda 21 and other initiatives and reviews the work to date on sustainability supported by the Local Government Management Board (1994, 1995a, 1995b). Despite considerable technical progress in developing indicators and in testing them for acceptability to the public, there is not much evidence of this work bearing fruit in terms of policy appraisal and policy design for sustainability. He suggests, as did Bruder in Chapter 2, that the context of policy making in local government may not be conducive to such changes and that education and awareness raising may be required. He goes on to suggest that the relationship of trust between the community and local government has broken down. The public is unlikely to be mobilised into supporting environmental action by expert opinion in local government (or elsewhere) and the development of policy needs to be more of 'an exercise in information, negotiation, deliberation and consensus building with the population'.

Dominic Stead's contribution looks at environmental indicators and targets for more sustainable land use plans. He says that the derivation of environmental targets and indicators should follow on from the definition of sustainability objectives. They can play a part at various stages of the policy-implementation process - policy development, policy appraisal, policy implementation, policy assessment/review - but have a particular value in focusing attention on the link between the policy implementation process and outcomes. But the process of target setting is political as well as it is scientific. Quoting Jacobs (1993) he suggests that environmental targets cannot be set by the 'facts' of scientific analysis alone. The values of society and the goals it wants to set for current and future generations have to be reflected too. Land use plans are beginning to incorporate environmental targets and judging by an evaluation of the success of target setting in local road safety policies in Norway (Elvik 1993), the adoption of quantitative and ambitious targets are likely to lead to more effective action than the setting of qualitative and less ambitious targets. Yet it has to be recognised in setting targets that some targets are easier to achieve than others. What might look like an ambitious target in one sector in relation to carbon dioxide emissions may be easy to achieve because the underlying trend has been downward, compared with another less apparently ambitious target in a sector where emissions have been growing.

One of the key concepts in the development of more formal techniques of policy evaluation is the notion of environmental capacity. Arguments over environmental capacity are being used increasingly to justify constraints on settlement pattern and urban form. But as Hugh Barton points out in Chapter 6 there is as yet no generally accepted and robust technique for the definition of capacity and he suggests that the concept as currently applied is dangerous because it tends to be partial and open to hijacking by specific interests. He criticises the approaches of some planning authorities who treat all open land as 'critical environmental capacity' and therefore sacrosanct. Equally he is critical of the urban study of Chester (Ove Arup 1993), which uses both physical and perceptual measures of overcrowding of open spaces, streets, pedestrian areas to assess capacity but includes some consideration of aesthetics and socio-economic issues. This is partial, Barton concludes, because it concentrates on local environmental quality at the expense of the impacts on neighbouring areas and at the possible expense of global resources. His alternative approach stresses the need for a comprehensive view of capacity in relation to all elements of environmental stock, and a recognition that sustainable development - not purely environmental sustainability - demands explicit treatment of social, economic, global and local environmental priorities. Applying these arguments to the debate about urban form and the compact city leads Barton to conclude that the practical and 'environmentally sound' alternative to compact cities or new settlements is continued suburban development, a view that Winter and Farthing share in Chapter 10.

Chapters 7 and 8 are both concerned with public support for environmental policy and therefore in a democratic society with the legitimacy of environmental policy. Local Agenda 21 stresses that this legitimacy must come from consultation with citizens. Thus the evaluation of environmental policies is concerned as much with the process that is established between local government, local groups and the local population as it is with the product of that process. Given the neglect of public opinion in much local government policy-making and the inadequacy of the methods that have been adopted to allow public input into decision-making, such consultation requires for many local authorities the creation of new institutional arrangements. Tessa Coombes and Martin Fodor point out in Chapter 7 on the basis of their case study of Bristol that whilst there is evidence of public interest in contributing to LA21 processes, such developments in consultation require resources, organisation and commitment (from both central and local government). It is perhaps not surprising therefore that few authorities appear to be engaged in developing new consultation procedures for LA21.

But the importance of new consultative mechanisms are highlighted by the research of Tony Harrison reported in Chapter 8. He evaluates the mechanisms of the land use planning system, arguably those that have presented the greatest opportunities for local involvement in environmental issues. He raises three important questions and draws on research carried out for the Department of the Environment (McCarthy and Harrison 1995) on public attitudes to planning to answer them. First, does the system provide clear signals about the public's aspirations for environmental outcomes? He is doubtful about this. Whilst there is evidence that people want the planning system to protect the countryside and create a healthy environment, there is widespread ignorance of the role of local politicians in decision-making and, interestingly, given the discussion of environmental appraisal in Chapter 3, of the development plan system. People seem to lack the knowledge that would enable them to communicate their feelings to local government. Second, does the system provide guidance on the trade-offs that are acceptable in moving towards those ends? Once again he concludes that it provides limited guidance given the level of knowledge of opportunities to influence the decision and the greater likelihood of involvement by those negatively affected by proposals at the decision stage. Third, does the public have confidence in the legitimacy of the process of making environmental decisions? Harrison also has his doubts here. The system appear to be viewed as an adversarial one which is less concerned with finding the best location for develop than a site-by-site battle on specific proposals. The consideration of the full environmental impacts of decisions would also seem to be limited by the definition of what are appropriate planning matters, restricting consideration to land use implications. It may be however that Harrison's respondents were reflecting a period of planning history before the wide range of environmental issues appropriate to land use planning (discussed in Chapter 3 by Baker) were introduced into policy guidance.

The impact of policies, programmes and initiatives after they have been implemented is the subject of summative evaluation examples of which are discussed in Chapter 9 on park and ride schemes and Chapter 10 on neighbourhood planning policies. This type of policy evaluation represents the traditional concern of evaluation assessing the benefits that have accrued from the adoption of the policy, programme or initiative in relation to the goals set for it. Impact evaluations raise at least two important methodological questions for the evaluator. First, what are the environmental outcomes which the policy is intended to achieve? Policies and proposals rarely have single, unambiguous objectives. Instead reflecting the political processes of negotiation and bargaining involved in their creation, they often have very vaguely stated goals (which is true of park and ride schemes). In the case of neighbourhood planning it is not clear that they ever had very strong environmental goals at all and the task of the evaluator is to define post hoc measures of impact. This of course emphasises the benefits of clarity in spelling out the meaning of sustainable development through the development of indicators and targets. Second, how can the impact of the policy be measured in a way which allows the impact of all other factors to be controlled? How do we know what would have happened in the absence of the policy? This leads back to the debate raised earlier about the methodology of evaluation and the importance in some analysts view of basing work on the logic of experimental methods.

A policy that has been widely advocated and increasingly adopted for combatting urban congestion and producing environmental benefits is park and ride, particularly bus based schemes. By 1993 sixteen schemes were operating year round on a six day week basis. Another 25 towns and cities were operating a seasonal or Saturday only scheme. Whilst there has been some opposition to such schemes on the grounds of their impact on town centre economic activity (quoted for example in Hill and Smith 1994), Geoff Mills points out in Chapter 9 that the benefits of such schemes in terms of developing sustainable transport strategies have been largely unquestioned. Using a case study of a park and ride scheme in Bristol, Mills reports on an evaluation of the success of the scheme in saving fuel use. His main findings are that the provision of park and ride on corridors that already have extensive public transport services is likely to produce a level of abstraction from the existing services that could negate any environmental benefits achieved by the attraction of former car users. His conclusions are that where schemes are introduced it is desirable to avoid such corridors but unfortunately these are the very corridors which would have sufficient demand to justify introducing the scheme. Attention needs to be given therefore both to the relative price and quality of services to minimise abstraction and to measures for restraining car use in the area. His final judgement is that except where it would be very costly to provide public transport, it would be preferable on both environmental and social grounds if travellers could be persuaded to make the whole journey by public transport. Not only would this conserve resources and reduce pollution but the additional demand and level of services provided would benefit all travellers, not just those with access to a car.

John Winter and Stuart Farthing look at the renewed interest of government policy in neighbourhood planning which they suggest in Chapter 10, had fallen from official grace in planning orthodoxy by the 1970s. A key dimension of neighbourhood planning is the provision of facilities to be provided with new housing development. Planning Policy Guidance Note 13 (PPG13) refers to the need in the context of reducing greenhouse gas emissions from the transport sector to plan for the local provision of facilities for everyday activities. This will it is asserted reduce the demand for travel, and the use of the car. Indeed, PPG13 makes some quite strong claims about the relationship between the local provision of facilities and services and the increased use of walking and cycling. This is in line with what might be described as the conventional wisdom amongst transport planners that accessibility is an important determinant of travel behaviour. Based on their research on 5 large housing developments with different levels of local facility provision, they found varying levels of use of local facilities but local provision did lead to a significant reduction in the length of journeys by car. Local provision however was not enough to have a significant impact on the decision to walk to the local facility. They conclude that there is a significant contribution to be made towards sustainability from the integrated provision of facilities and new housing development. And this is important they point out because it is unrealistic and undesirable to accommodate all new housing within existing built-up areas. They advocate therefore a recognition of the need for continued peripheral development appropriately planned and coordinated. In order to encourage more walking and cycling to local facilities and services they suggest that an approach that focusses specifically on design in favour of pedestrian movement is required which minimises pedestrian journeys, provides high amenity footpaths or cycleways within networks of high quality open spaces, providing direct access to centres.

In Chapter 11 Richard Guise investigates the neglected topic of paving and its use by local government as part of strategies to protect and revitalize town centres. Unlike policies for park and ride and for neighbourhood planning discussed in the previous chapters, no real connection has been made between environmental outcomes and the floorscape of the public realm though dissatisfaction with current practice has been growing. Guise sets out to show that the use of traditional paving (ie natural stone rather than concrete and tarmac) can be a more 'sustainable' solution. Not only does it contribute to local distinctiveness and character of small towns but natural stone has a longer life, can be re-used and the manufacturing and laying process uses less energy. Any expansion of the use of natural stone is unlikely to have major environmental impacts on the landscape since expansion can be accommodated by using beds in existing quarries, and re-opening former quarries. If new quarries are needed they will be small-scale, efficiently worked (all stone can be used) and will cause less nuisance than aggregate quarrying since less machinery is needed and less noise, dust and visual intrusion is created.

References

Agyeman, J. and Evans, B. (eds)(1994), *Local Environmental Policies and Strategies*, Longman: Harlow.

Biddick, I. (1995), 'Sustainable development indicators project: seattle USA' *BURISA* 118, pp. 9-12.

Blowers, A. (1993), 'Environmental policy: the quest for sustainable development' *Urban Studies*, Vol 30, NO 4/5, pp. 775-796.

Carley, M. and Christie, I. (1992), *Managing sustainable development*, Earthscan: London.

Cook, T.D., and Campbell, D.T. (1979), *Quasi-Experimentation Design and Analysis Issues for Field Settings*, Rand McNally: Skokie, IL.

Cronbach, L.J. (1982), *Designing Evaluations of Educational and Social Programs*, Jossey-Bass: San Francisco.

Coombes, T. Farthing, S. Winter, J. (1990), *An Assessment of Growth Sector Policy in the Borough of Eastleigh* Planning and Environment Research Unit, Faculty of the Built Environment, UWE, Bristol.

Department of the Environment (1993), *Environmental Appraisal of Development Plans: A Good Practice Guide*, HMSO: London.

Elvik, R. (1993), 'Quantified Road Safety Targets' *Accident Analysis and Prevention* Vol.25, No.5. pp. 569-583.

Friend, J.K. and Jessop, W.N. (1977), *Local Government and Strategic Choice*, Pergamon: Oxford.

Golding, A. (1994), 'Empowerment and decentralisation', in Agyeman, J. and Evans, B. (eds) *Local Environmental Policies and Strategies*, Longman: Harlow.

Hams, T., Jacobs, M., Levett, R. Lusser, H., Morphet, J ., Taylor, D. (1994), *Greening Your Local Authority* Longman: Harlow.

Hill, D. and Smith,T. (1994), 'Environmental management and audit', in Agyeman, J. and Evans, B. (eds) *Local Environmental Policies and Strategies* Longman: Harlow.

Hope, C. and Parker, J. (1995), 'Environmental Indices for France, Italy and the UK', *European Environment*, Vol. 5, pp. 13-19.

Jacobs, M. (1993), *Sense and Sustainability*, Council for the Protection of Rural England: London.

Jacobs, M. (1994), 'The Limits To Neoclassicism: Towards An Institutional Environmental Economics' in Redclift, M. and Benton, T. (eds) *Social Theory and the Global Environment* Routledge: London.

Janowitz, M.(1992), *Sociological Models and Social Policy*, General Learning Systems: Morristown NJ.

Local Authorities Research and Intelligence Association (1995), *National Review of the Role of Research in Local Government*, Local Government Management Board: Luton.

Local Government Management Board (1993), *UK Local Government Declaration on Sustainable Development*, Local Government Management Board: Luton.

Local Government Management Board, United Nations Association, Touche Ross (1994), *The Sustainability Indicators Research Project: Report of Phase One*, Local Government Management Board: Luton.

Local Government Management Board, United Nations Association, Touche Ross (1995a), *The Sustainability Indicators Research Project; Guidance to Pilot Authorities*, Local Government Management Board: Luton.

Local Government Management Board, United Nations Association, Touche Ross (1995b), *The Sustainability Indicators Research Project; Report of Phase Two.* Local Government Management Board: Luton.

Marshall, T. (1994), 'British Planning and the New Environmentalism' *Planning Practice and Research*, Vol. 9, No. 1, pp. 21-30.

McCarthy, P. and Harrison, A.R. (1995), *Attitudes to Town and Country Planning* Department of the Environment Planning Research Programme HMSO: London.

Nakamura, R.T. and Smallwood, F. (1980), *The Politics of Policy Implementation*, St. Martin's Press: New York.

Ove Arup and Partners in association with Breheny, M., Donald W. Insall and Associates, DTZ Debenham Thorpe (1993) *Environmental Capacity and Development in Historic Cities*, for Cheshire County Council, Chester City Council, Department of the Environment, and English Heritage.

Palumbo, D.J. (ed.)(1987), *The Politics of Program Evaluation* Sage: Newbury Park.

Patton, M. Q. (1986), *Utilization-focused Evaluation*, Sage: Beverley Hills, CA.

Pearce, D., Turner, R., Brown, D., and Bateman, I. (1991), *The Development of Environmental Indicators*, Report to the DoE, University College London.

Rees, S. and Wehrmeyer,W. (1995), *Issues in Implementation of Sustainable Development Strategies for the UK Local Government Context, Crisis of Definition, Identity, Resources and Authority,* Research Paper to 1995 International Sustainable Development Conference, Manchester 1995.

Rist, R. C. (ed) (1995), *Policy Evaluation: Linking Theory to Practice* Edward Elgar: Aldershot.

Rosenhead, J. (ed) (1989), *Rational Analysis for a Problematic World*, Wiley: Chichester.

Rossi, P. H. and Freeman, H.E. (1989), *Evaluation. A Systematic Approach*, Sage: Newbury Park, CA.

Selman, P. (1995), 'Local sustainability', *Town Planning Review*, Vol. 66, No. 3, pp. 287-301.

Schon, D. A. (1983), *The Reflective Practitioner: How Professionals Think in Action*, Temple Smith: London.

Stoker, G. and Young, S. (1993), *Cities in the 1990s*, Longman: Harlow.

United Nations Conference on Environment and Development (1993), *Earth Summit Agenda 21: the United Nations Programme of Action from Rio*, United Nations Department of Public Information: New York.

Ward, S. (1993), 'Thinking global, acting local? Local authorities and their environmental plans', *Environmental Politics*, II, 30.

Webber, P. (1994), 'Environmental Strategies' in Agyeman,J. and Evans,B. (eds) *Local Environmental Policies and Strategies*, Longman: Harlow.

Whittaker, S. (1995), 'Local Agenda 21 and local authorities' *Local Government Policy Making*, Vol.22,No.2, pp. 3-11.

Wilson, E. (1993), *Strategic Environmental Assessment*, Earthscan: London.

World Commission on Environment and Development (1987), *Our Common Future*, Oxford University Press: Oxford.

2 Lessons from environmental auditing for the development of local environmental policy

Noel Bruder

Introduction

The process of environmental auditing (EA) gained widespread usage and recognition in UK local government in the early 1990's. Opinions as to what is and what is not included within the concept of EA vary but it is generally considered to encompass an element of review and of strategic policy making with the overall goal of improving environmental performance.

For many local authorities their initial phase of EA represented their first attempt at developing a comprehensive environmental strategy. This is to say that, EA has moved local government environmental policy making beyond a limited sectoral focus; has sought to instil environmental principles as core elements in local government decision making: and has sought to integrate policy areas, professional disciplines and different agencies. Although these characteristics are not present in all EA processes, they represent qualities which can be engendered.

The experience gained from managing EA is now being applied in a number of related environmental initiatives, principally Local Agenda 21 strategies and environmental management systems.

Through an evaluation of the experience of local authorities with the application of EA, this chapter will assess the implications and lessons for the future development of local government's capacity for environmental management.

The meaning of environmental auditing

There are many different perspectives on the EA process. Most, however, involve a distinction between *Internal Auditing (IA)* and *State of the Environment reporting (SoE)* such as the following by ACC, ADC, AMA (1990):

- IA: 'A review of the environmental impact of policies and practices and of measures needed to reduce or eliminate any detrimental activities'

- SoE: 'A comprehensive appraisal of the condition of the overall environment, based on a continually up-dated database.'

While the concept of SoE reporting is relatively straight forward, IA combines a number of related activities. These may be sub-divided as follows:

- *Policy Impact Assessment (PIA)* - an assessment of the policies of a local authority, not just in environmental areas but in all sectors. This concerns the environmental impacts of the authority in its role as regulator, enforcer, enabler, educator and service provider. The PIA should lead to a revision of strategic policies.
- *Review of Internal Practices (RIP)* - an examination of the internal practices of a local authority, from the point of view of their environmental significance and impact and how these could be improved.
- *Management Audit (MA)* - this is similar to a RIP but focuses specifically on organisational structures and culture, the co-ordination of policies and practices, the allocation of responsibilities and resources and the methods of communication.

These elements are combined within the process of EA in order that a local authority can move from policy formation to action implementation. A basic framework for how the elements may be combined is shown in Figure 2.1.

Procedures and management

The discussion so far should demonstrate, firstly, the potential complexity and contribution of EA and, secondly, the range of perspectives which are encompassed within the process of EA. As a first step to examining the alternative approaches which have been adopted by local authorities, Figure 2.2 presents a theoretical model for viewing the EA process. The quadrant, combining a policy process dimension with an institutional arrangements dimension, facilitates a more detailed analysis of EA than if only one dimension were examined. The main components in each perspective are outlined below:

A *functional* approach is associated with a technical application of the elements in a process, with an emphasis on activities rather than institutional arrangements.

A *strategic* approach has as a goal policy integration and the achievement of a coherent process of environmental management. It emphasises political as well as technical aspects and takes account of the institutional realities associated with goal formation, decision making and implementation.

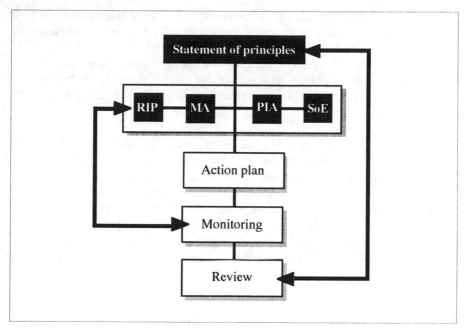

Figure 2.1   The basic framework for an environmental auditing process

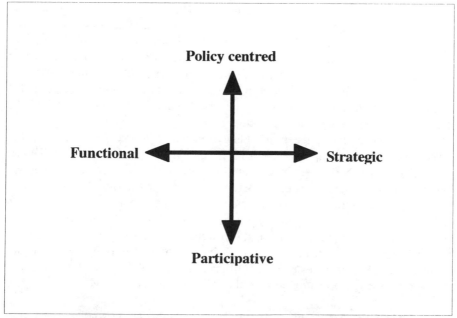

Figure 2.2   A theoretical model for viewing the environmental auditing process

A *policy centred* approach is associated here with a hierarchical view of management and a technocratic application of processes. Command and control are defining characteristics.

A *participative* approach seeks to achieve interaction and collaboration between the different agents involved in a process. It emphasises organisational culture, the management of change and the characteristics of ownership, commitment and awareness.

Applying this model to an analysis of current EA activities highlights a number of important issues. In relation to the policy process dimension, the emphasis to date has been to advocate a strategic view but for actual practice to be more functional. This is partly an issue of environmental complexity. The issues addressed in EA are not amenable to simple solutions and a local authority is thus often left grappling with these complexities and unable to fulfil strategic goals. The emphasis on a functional approach is also due to the relative novelty of the EA process. Techniques, knowledge and expertise are still developing but are as yet often not capable of fulfilling the strategic aspirations set for the process. Thus, the initial phases of EA are part of a learning exercise. The fruits of this labour are yet to be fully realised.

In relation to the institutional arrangements dimension, the key point is that most of the current approaches have been predominantly policy centred rather than participative. Thus they have been internal to the local authority and have been managed in a traditional, hierarchical, fashion. The reasons for this approach are partly the same as those outlined above. In addition, there have been difficulties in demarcating environmental rights and responsibilities. This has been particularly evident between certain functional areas and professional responsibilities within local authorities and in the problems of co-ordinating multi-agency initiatives. The problems in achieving a participative approach have been added to by the expanded agenda of sustainable development and the concomitant enlargement of the identifiable community interests.

On a theoretical level, the key finding from current practice is that the EA process is viewed and approached from a rational perspective. This has helped popularise and provided legitimacy for the process. The systematic procedures, logical analysis, assumptions of institutional capacity and normative framework advocated by the rational approach have enabled EA to be accommodated within current local authority structures and have facilitated an exchange of experience and prescriptions for how to proceed. However, the limitations of this type of approach have been widely recognised in the literature (see, for example, Hambleton, 1986; Benveniste, 1989; Hill and Smith, 1994). These limitations, as they apply to EA, are centred around the following points:

- The environmental and institutional complexities are downplayed.
- Comprehensive knowledge and coverage are assumed but are in reality impossible.

- Lack of resources and powers limit what is currently possible.
- Widespread participation is inhibited and ownership is not enhanced.

The key to overcoming these limitations is to combine the advantages offered by the rational approach with an appreciation of the context in which the process is operating. This is the focus of the discussion which follows.

A strategic framework for environmental auditing

The full potential of EA would appear to lie in the expanded, strategic, view of the process. Not only does this incorporate a broader range of tasks and perspectives but it provides the basis for an integrated system of environmental management in local government.

Figure 2.3 presents a framework which combines and shows some of the relationships between EA elements. Each of the main elements or tasks in this framework will be discussed below. It is not possible in this short chapter to provide a detailed analysis of each of the stages in the EA process and all the relevant institutional arrangements. A more comprehensive discussion can be found in Barton and Bruder (1995). The discussion here focuses on broadly defined tasks.

The most basic EA task is that of *review*. All audits must start from a baseline of knowledge of where the local authority stands in relation to the various environmental issues being considered, current practices, policy responses and, depending on the scope of the process, the current state of the local environment. This involves a functional application of auditing procedures and leads to a description of current activities. For some authorities, EA does not extend beyond this task. The audit is viewed as a relatively limited policy instrument which is used in support of management functions.

A development from a basic review is where the information gained is then subject to a more detailed *assessment* in order to evaluate current performance and direct future action. This is obviously a more onerous task, needing greater time and expertise. The output, however, should be more valuable. It takes a local authority beyond what it currently does and is the first step to defining a coherent environmental strategy. There are several qualities which should be striven for in an assessment. First, it should be realistic in its coverage. The scope of interest is potentially limitless so the issues of greatest concern should be prioritised early on. At the same time, the interrelationships between issues should be highlighted and the audit should maintain a strategic overview. This twin requirement dictates that there should be different levels operating simultaneously in the EA process. An on-going programme of detailed assessment could be accompanied by a more widespread but partial assessment of the entire range of issues.

A second important quality is that of objectivity. This relates to the definition of targets and indicators and the assessment methods used. Targets and indicators are essential for refining the operational objectives of the EA process. As the degree

Task	Description	Designation
Review	Policy instrument/management tool	Functional
	Essentially descriptive	
Assessment	Evaluation of performance	
	Guiding future action	
		Normative
Decision making	To consider environmental implications in the political process	
Ownership	To promote involvement and awareness	
		Institutional
Organisational change	To develop the capacity to adapt to change	

Figure 2.3 The strategic framework of environmental auditing

of analytical rigor demanded from EA has increased, local authorities are having to be more diligent in applying explicit assessment criteria. Similarly, the assessment methods used are gradually becoming more advanced, particularly through the use of comparative matrices. What is most important, however, is that the search for objectivity does not obscure the essentially subjective nature of many of the issues being assessed. This subjectivity should be highlighted and not hidden. So, while the best practical method should be employed and detailed assessment criteria applied where possible, the emphasis should be on maintaining transparency and participation.

A final assessment quality which needs to be highlighted is the detailed specification of recommendations for action. Achieving environmental and institutional change should provide the focus for EA and every effort must therefore be put into ensuring that recommendations are capable of being implemented. An important part of this is that they are presented in a form and format which facilitates application. Thus, the budgeting, timescale, prioritisation and allocation of responsibilities should be worked out in as much detail as possible.

The output from the assessment is only useful if it is fed into the wider local authority management system. This is the role of EA in *decision making*. EA must seek to influence decision making systems so that the environmental implications of policies and practices are considered in the local authority political process. Environmental concerns should be integrated with and considered alongside other sectoral interests. In order to facilitate this there needs to be a realistic and honest statement of the aims of EA and an understanding of the resource commitments involved. Too often the high aspirations of EA are lost when these are found to conflict with more established local authority interest (such as economic development) or when the full implications of what is involved becomes realised.

Another important factor in decision making is the achievement of a consensual approach. Choices of aims, objectives, recommendations, etc. refine the options open to EA and therefore represent decision points. The process must be developed in such a way as to promote involvement and consensual agreement. This is a function of the institutional tasks of EA which are discussed next.

EA can not be viewed solely as a technical environmental process. The changes which are sought are as much in perceptions, motivations and behaviour as they are in refinements in policy and practice. An essential task of EA is therefore to generate *ownership* of the process through the promotion of involvement and awareness. As discussed earlier, the relatively formal and hierarchical approaches to management adopted thus far by local authorities have not necessarily highlighted the importance of ownership. Some attempts have been made to manage EA on an interdepartmental basis, specifically through the establishment of a dedicated officers steering group. Likewise, many authorities have seen the value of promoting community involvement through the use of environmental forums. These arrangements should be further developed and other mechanisms for direct involvement in EA explored. By being part of the process individuals, both in the authority and in the community, will become more aware of their roles and responsibilities and should as a result be more supportive of the aims of EA. This is particularly important with regard to those charged with implementing the recommendations which result from the audit.

Linked to the issue of ownership is the need to address *organisational change*. The culture which predominates in local government is not one which easily accommodates the type of fundamental changes which EA promotes. The institutional capacity of local authorities must therefore be developed in order to cultivate a culture of change. This requires that EA be built on a firm commitment from the members and high ranking officers within local authorities. It also requires that EA be developed as a corporate initiative and be seen as the responsibility of all sections of the local authority. One specific aspect of change which should be sought is for the local authority to adopt a more participative approach through multi-agency working and community involvement.

The final element shown in Figure 2.3 is the *implementation* of actions in order to achieve tangible benefits. In a sense, this is a product of all the other tasks. Effective implementation should provide the focus for the development of the EA process. While the use of explicit targets and indicators will facilitate the assessment of implementation effectiveness these should not be considered in isolation. More intangible criteria, such as perceptional changes and levels of involvement, should also be considered. The assessment of effectiveness will require that systems for monitoring and review are developed as an integral part of the EA process and that management have a commitment to act on the findings.

The discussion in this section has expanded on the main elements in a strategic EA process. It has been suggested that this strategic process offers a system which combines the advantages of a rational approach with an appreciation of the environmental and institutional context within which EA is operating. Some recommendations have been made for achieving the full potential from this expanded view of EA.

The next section will briefly explore the future potential of EA and the implications for local government environmental management.

Future potential of environmental auditing and implications for local government environmental management

The majority of local authorities have now completed the first phase of their EA process. Many have developed quite comprehensive and multi-layered approaches and have successfully integrated EA activities with other aspects of local authority work, such as in education and economic development. The most notable factor in relation to current approaches to EA is that the elements in the process have undergone considerable fragmentation and reformation. Thus, it is no longer common to refer to EA as a single process with the component elements of PIA, RIP, MA and SoE reporting. Figure 2.4 gives some idea of the range of activities

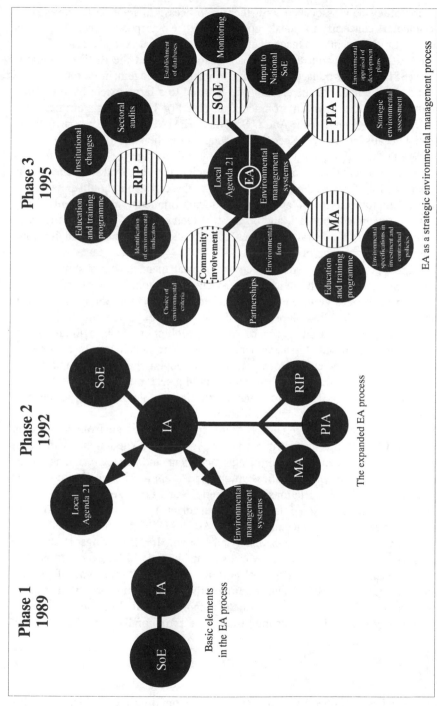

Phase 1
1989

Basic elements
in the EA process

Phase 2
1992

The expanded EA process

Phase 3
1995

EA as a strategic environmental management process

Figure 2.4   Phases in the development of the environmental auditing process

27

and terminology now associated with the EA process. In relation to the current environmental concerns in local government, two aspects are particularly important: Environmental Management Systems and Local Agenda 21.

In the last two years both the European Union (EU) and the British Standards Institute (BSI) have introduced formal environmental management systems. These systems duplicate many of the elements in EA and to a large extent have become synonymous with the term 'environmental audit'. For UK local government, the EU's 'Eco-Management and Audit Scheme' (EMAS) has been particularly influential because it has been specifically adapted for their use (DoE and LGMB, 1993). While the full significance of environmental management systems has yet to be realised, there are some comments which can be made based on the experience of EA. First, and on the positive side, these systems should enhance the coherence and objectivity of approaches to environmental management. They advocate an integrated approach and because of their general application they will allow comparisons to be drawn between local authorities. This should improve expertise and an exchange of experience.

The biggest potential problem with environmental management systems is that they advocate an extremely rational approach. The problems with an overtly rational approach were noted earlier and the implication is that the advantages of a strategic and participative approach will be lost through the promotion of a functional and policy centred approach. Another problem noted by Hill and Smith (1994) is that environmental management systems were developed for application in the private sector, where performance can be judged against sales and profit. They are therefore unsuitable for use in the public sector where performance is more difficult to assess. These problems are not intractable but the experience of EA suggests that a cautionary approach should be taken.

While environmental management systems appear to diverge from a strategic approach to EA the opposite is true of Local Agenda 21. The emphasis in Local Agenda 21 is on consensus building, empowerment and strategic management. These are some of the characteristics which current approaches to EA most need to enhance. The reciprocal relationship between EA and Local Agenda 21 is clearly evident in the advice offered to local government for how to proceed with producing strategies (see, for example, LGMB, 1994). This emphasises all the tasks shown in Figure 2.3 and discussed above. It also brings sustainable development to the forefront of the environmental agenda in local government.

Given the lack of expertise that local authorities have with the type of process advocated by Local Agenda 21 and the imperative of producing an initial strategy by the end of 1996, it is clear that local authorities will draw heavily on the experience they have gained over the last five years in conducting EA.

Conclusions

This chapter has examined some of the issues surrounding the application of EA in UK local government. The discussion has highlighted a number of procedural and institutional limitations which will need to be overcome if the full potential of environmental management processes is to be realised. The strategic framework for EA presented in Figure 2.3 incorporates a range of tasks which an integrated approach to environmental management should focus on. Whether directly through EA or through associated processes, the future of local government environmental policy lies in a strategic and participative approach.

References

Association of County Councils (ACC), Association of District Councils (ADC), Association of Metropolitan Authorities (AMA) (1990) *Environmental Practice in Local Government. First edition* ACC: London

Barton, H. and Bruder, N. (1995), *A Guide to Local Environmental Auditing*, Earthscan: London

Benveniste, G, (1989), *Mastering the Politics of Planning*, Jossey-Bass: Oxford

Department of the Environment (DoE) and Local Government Management Board (LGMB) (1993), *A Guide to the Eco-Management and Audit Scheme for UK Local Government*, HMSO: London

Hambleton, R. (1986), *Rethinking Policy Planning*, School for Advanced Urban Studies: Bristol

Hill, D. and Smith, T. (1994), 'Environmental Management and Auditing' in: Agyeman, J. and Evans, B. (eds.) *Local Environmental Policies and Strategies*, Longman: London

Local Government Management Board (1994), *A Step by Step Guide to Local Agenda 21*, LGMB: Luton

3 Environmental appraisal of development plans

John Baker

Introduction

This chapter addresses the central theme of the book: how can policy making, in this case in development plans, more fully engage with the environmental imperative that is essential in moving towards sustainability. It introduces the relatively new process of environmental appraisal in development plans by considering why it has come into use, and by explaining the intended approach. The chapter then proceeds to examine some of the limitations in practice to date and ends by proposing what might be the full potential for environmental appraisal.

Changes in the planning system

The environmental appraisal of development plans has emerged as the product of two distinct strands of change. The first is the changed significance of development plans in the town and country planning system. Since 1990 there is a requirement that a land use plan be prepared covering the whole of the area administered by a district or borough council to include site specific proposals. This may be a local plan, functioning within the strategic overview of the structure plan prepared for the county, or it may be a unitary development plan, where the strategic and local policies are combined in one document.

This requirement was followed, by way of encouragement to the plan makers perhaps, with the introduction by statute of the concept of 'primacy' for the development plan. Whereas the development plan, where it existed in a credible form, was previously one consideration in determining a planning application, it became from 1991 onwards the first consideration. When the plan is adopted, and when there are relevant policies, a planning application is to be determined in accordance with the plan unless material considerations indicate otherwise[1].

Planning authorities and the development industry are still learning what to do with this power and what it means. The first round of plans to benefit from this role is still in production. In 1990 it was envisaged that full coverage of adopted local plans and UDPs would be achieved by 1996 (UK Government 1996). This will certainly not be the case, with plans taking far longer to produce than was hoped or foreseen. The importance now attached to development plans is almost certainly one reason for the time being taken.

The second vital change is the introduction of the idea of sustainability and sustainable development, and the adoption of the latter by the town and country planning system. The UK government declared its commitment to sustainable development in 1990 with the publication of the White Paper 'This Common Inheritance'(UK Government 1990). Here it is said that:

> The Government therefore supports the principle of sustainable development. this means living on the earth's income rather than eroding its capital. It means keeping the consumption of renewable natural resources within the limits of their replenishment. It means handing down to successive generations not only man-made wealth (such as buildings, roads and railways) but also natural wealth, such as clean and adequate water supplies, good arable land, a wealth of wildlife and ample forests.

Land use planning is well placed to take on board the ideas of sustainable development. It is about making provision for homes, business space and infrastructure - meeting our needs - and it is about protecting the environment that we value. It is about finding a balance when these objectives conflict. Unusually for public policy making town planning has developed procedures to enable the public to influence choices and decisions at a local level. At its best planning involves thinking about the way in which we should live in the future, so that if we are to move towards sustainability the planning system has a part to play.

The Government said as much in with the publication of PPG12: Development Plans and Regional Planning Guidance (DoE 1992b, para. 1.8). This says that:

> The planning system, and the preparation of development plans in particular, can contribute to the objectives of ensuring that development and growth are sustainable. The sum total of decision in the planning field, as elsewhere, should not deny future generations the best of today's environment.

The introduction of sustainable development into development planning has had consequences which are still to be fully realised. It has arguably gained for planning a mission or purpose which it has lacked. All of the issues which planning decisions must consider are aligned in one direction by the goal of sustainable development, or they are subordinated to this overarching consideration. That is how the consequences of sustainable development are seen by some.

Alternatively the all embracing nature of sustainable development is seen as the weakness of the concept. To do almost anything, or absolutely nothing, can be presented as 'the sustainable way', and either side in a planning conflict may call upon the concept of sustainable development for support. This is particularly so because the meaning of sustainable development embraces economic ideas. It does so, rightly, by embracing a commitment to fairness and equity. More often in planning situations however it is argued by developers, or by planning authorities justifying the use of land for employment purposes, that only if there are jobs will the well being of a community be maintained, and environmental measures be afforded. Some of the difficulties that the pursuit of sustainable development through land use planning will have to overcome have been set out by the author elsewhere (Baker 1995).

The breadth of environmental issues

A particular consequence of linking sustainable development to land use planning has been to draw new environmental issues into consideration. PPG12 (DoE 1992 b, para 6.5) identifies some of these, requiring development plans to take into account for instance:

* sustaining the character and diversity of the countryside and undeveloped waste;
* conservation of the built and archaeological heritage;
* the best use of mineral resources;
* the reduction of CO_2 emissions;
* energy conservation, and the opportunities for renewable energy;
* wildlife conservation;
* impact upon landscape quality;
* environmental health considerations;
* the improvement of the physical environment;
* the protection of groundwater resources.

The significant point here is the number of environmental considerations, and their diversity. The integrity of the ozone layer or the composition of the atmosphere are issues which are quite different in nature to, say, the conservation of a listed building. A change to atmospheric composition is several stages removed from the type of issue over which the planning process has jurisdiction. The link to the planning system, and hence the justification for the atmosphere as a legitimate planning consideration, can be expressed as follows:

* global warming has negative implications for human occupation of the planet
* gaseous emissions to the atmosphere contribute to global warming
* one cause of greenhouse gases is the burning of fossil fuels
* fossil fuels are burnt in the provision of transport
* one factor in determining demand for transport is the relationship between land

uses
- the planning system has some influence in the relationship between land uses

A link therefore exists between the integrity of the atmosphere and land use planning, and by such thinking the explicit scope and purpose of planning has been widened.

The emergence of environmental appraisal

Planning involves weighing together different considerations and making choices, but it is difficult conceptually for the planning system to take on board such a large number and range of environmental issues.

The introduction of a wider range of environmental issues brings additional tensions and potentially greater conflict. Planning has tended to simplify conflicts into those between environmental, economic and social considerations, but sustainability has highlighted the presence of conflicts between different types of environmental issue. Conflicts occur, for instance, between issues which are essentially local and those which are global in nature. Local issues, the protection of a piece of open space for instance, are immediate and readily understood, whilst a concern such as that for the change to atmospheric conditions through CO_2 emissions is seen as very long term, difficult to comprehend, and remote. Planning can have a major impact on the former type of issue, but can only have a very tiny, and unquantifiable, impact on a very important issue in the latter example. The popular concern, and hence perhaps the political vote, lies with the former type of issue rather than the latter. Yet to move towards sustainability the one concern cannot always preclude consideration of the other. A systematic approach is needed to ensure that this is not the case, and if planning decisions are to be plan-led the place for this systematic review is in the formulation of the development plan. The need for some kind of appraisal emerges in PPG12 (DoE 1992 b) as a consequence of:

- the recognition of the breadth of environmental issues
- the acknowledgement that planning decisions have impact upon these issues
- the view that these impacts should be identified and taken into account in making choices.

PPG12 (DoE 1992 b, para. 6.1) identifies as a 'major responsibility' for local authorities that of ensuring that 'development plans are drawn up in such a way as to take environmental considerations comprehensively and consistently into account'. Environmental appraisal is now coming into more regular use in the preparation of development plans as a consequence of PPG12 and with the publication by the DoE (1993) of Good Practice Guidelines to assist with environmental appraisal (Therivel 1994).

In the Guidelines the environmental appraisal of development plans is described as 'an explicit, systematic and iterative review of development plan policies and proposals to evaluate their individual and combined impacts on the environment'(DoE 1993, p.2). The intentions of environmental appraisal are well described by the principles set out in the Guidelines. These are that environmental appraisal should be (DoE 1993, p.3):

simple in its concept, in its relationship with established planning practice and the planning process, and in its handling of information

transparent in its methodology and techniques, so that all involved can understand how and why policy and proposal options have been chosen

systematic so that it ensures that all aspects of the environment are considered

accommodating so that it is capable of entry at any level, depending on the history of plan making in the relevant area, and the skills, knowledge and resources available

flexible so that it is capable of informing decision making within whatever overall policy framework exists in, or is set by, the plan making body

progressive in that it can embrace additional and changing information and predictive techniques in an incremental way as knowledge and experience expand

consistent so that plans incorporating appraisal can link between tiered authorities, across plan making boundaries, and can interact usefully with the work of other agencies involved with environmental matters.

The preparation of the guide

At the time of PPG12 (DoE 1992 b) emerging however there was little to indicate how the appraisal now sought should be carried out. PPG12 makes reference to Policy Appraisal and the Environment (DoE 1991), as probably the only available publication addressing the issue, and a Government publication. This was apparently prepared for use in Government Departments, though evidence of its use in the formulation of policy is not known. It is useful in identifying the environmental issues that might be considered, presenting these in the form of checklists. But it did not provide a methodology for the environmental appraisal accessible to local authority planners or appropriate to the particular needs of development plans. Confronted with many requests for guidelines to be produced the DoE commissioned research into appraisal being undertaken by local planning authorities with a view to identifying and disseminating best practice (DoE 1993). The work was carried out by Baker Associates and the University of the West of England.

A survey of local planning authorities undertaken at the beginning of the research found relatively little work being done by way of formal appraisal. Some interesting work was underway in, for instance, Lancashire and Kent County

Councils, but there was no formal appraisal of a local plan along the lines envisaged by PPG12 identified by the survey (Lancashire County Council 1993; Kent County Council 1993).

In addition to the absence of guidelines (and in a very limited number of cases, the presence of a belief that appraisal was not a requirement applicable to their plan), the reasons generally given by local planning authorities for the absence of appraisal work on current plans were:

- the relative newness of the requirement, coupled with the stage already reached by the emerging plan
- the possibility that preparation of the plan would be delayed through the incorporation of appraisal
- a lack of the specialist skills assumed to be required and a general shortage of resources
- the belief that a plan whose content were angled more towards environmental concerns would not be supported when scrutinised by the DoE or if tested by an appeal.

The research did not rely entirely upon the existing work of local authorities in order to prepare a recommended approach to environmental appraisal. It also examined the literature upon decision making in planning, and upon the influence of environmental issues. An intensive process of consultation was undertaken to counsel the views of many organisations concerned with the relationship between planning and the environment, or which had views upon environmental appraisal.

Whilst very helpful in developing the proposals for the guidelines this wide consultation highlighted the unrealistic expectations held by some environmental groups about what the planning system can do, together with the conviction in this quarter that it should do more, by being more absolute in its protection of certain environmental features for instance

The researchers sought constantly to be aware of the particular nature of development plans, and to reflect in what was suggested the circumstances of most local authority planning departments.

The experience of environmental appraisal

The guidelines recommended a number of key tasks to be accomplished in the appraisal of development plans (DoE 1993, para. 2.4). These are:

- it must *'characterise the environment'* looking at key assets, threats and opportunities in order to provide a 'baseline' and context for considering the environmental effects of policies;
- it must *ensure that the scope of the plan covers the appropriate range of environmental concerns* in order to secure consideration of appropriate policy

and/or proposal options and to prevent emissions;
- it must *appraise policies and proposals to establish their environmental effects*; this is an iterative task which involves refinement, improvement and, if appropriate, development of policy/propoasl options which strive to remove inherent conflict within the plan; it will take place at several stages of plan making.

As an example of this process in use, the appraisal undertaken of the Consultation Draft of the Northavon Local Plan (1994) applies the majority of these steps.

Valuable experience on the evolving approach to environmental appraisal in development plans is provided by the work of Mendip District Council. Mendip District Council has demonstrated a commitment to 'green issues' which spans a number of aspects of its work, included the preparation of its development plan (Mendip District Council 1995, 1996). The Council has embarked upon a process of preparing its Local Plan which has utilised environmental appraisal from the outset. Great store has been placed upon the round table discussion of issues using the ideas of environmental appraisal to provide a structure; this was begun before policies have been drafted, and has involved people from beyond the planning department. This has meant the inclusion of the Council's environmental health and economic development officers and also of representatives of external bodies with different viewpoints and with specific expert knowledge of the environment, such as the NRA and the Countryside Commission.

Whilst Mendip District Council is an example of good practice, some other early examples of environmental appraisal emerging so far seem to pursue a mechanistic adherence to the minimum interpretation of the recommended approach in the Guidelines. In such cases the published plan includes a set of matrices indicating by symbols the existence or otherwise of an impact that a policy of the plan would have upon an element of environmental stock, together with the direction of that impact.

The Local Plan by Mole Valley District Council (1996) in Surrey is an example this approach being taken. The appraisal is treated as a test of the environmental credentials of what the Council proposes to include in the plan, but there is no indication that appraisal has been a tool used in the formulation of the plan policies, as PPG12 and the Guidelines indicate as the requirement. The matrices are supplemented by a brief commentary upon the significance of the impacts indicated but the appraisal is not used explicitly in support of any of the policy choices made.

The use of environmental appraisal in development plans is continuing to develop, with examples of work taking varying approaches emerging on a regular basis. At the structure plan level the appraisal of Bedfordshire's Structure Plann 2011 provides a great deal of information on the use of indicators. At the local plan level the environmental appraisal of Hinckley and Bosworth Local Plan applies the appraisal process to the plan proposals in particular (Hinkley and Bosworth 1995).

The experience of the use of environmental appraisal in development plans so far appears to confirm the appropriateness and relevence of the principles set out in the Guide, and quoted above, though the way in which the appraisal is carried out is clearly likely to vary.

The use of environmental appraisal

Both PPG12 (DoE 1992 b) and the Good Practice Guide (DoE 1993) make it clear that the requirement upon plans, and hence upon planning authorities, is to demonstrate that environmental issues have been taken into account in the formulation of the plan. The way in which this is done is for the Council to determine, and perhaps to satisfy the Inquiry process upon, though the Guidelines provide some suggestions.

The hope however must be that rather than being treated as a necessary chore and a formality, appraisal can be a cost effective addition to the tools and processes used in preparing plans, leading to a plan which:

- is properly protective of environmental capital as well as making provision for necessary development requirements
- seeks to ensure that development that does take place is undertaken in a more sustainable way
- is clear on any harmful environmental implications of its policies, and on the way the achievement of other objectives justifies the acceptance of these impacts
- is strong generally upon the justification of the choices set out.

The way in which the appropriate approach to appraisal may develop from that suggested in the Guide is in adopting distinct approaches to different components of the plan. Using the preparation of a local plan as an illustration, the components would be the strategy, the proposals and the policies.

The strategy is that part of the plan which by reference to PPG12 (DoE 1992 b, para. 7.3) sets out the overall aims which determine the approach taken within the plan: 'Each plan should also include in the introduction a clear and concise statement of its main aims, objectives and targets, and the strategy for achieving them, having regard to the likely level of resources available, both public and private sector'.

The term 'policies' is intended to refer to those policies of the plan which seek to prevent development in certain areas, designate areas in which certain provisions will prevail, or identify types of development and activity which will be resisted or encouraged by the plan.

'Proposals' are meant as those policies which, with the proposals map, allocate specific sites for specific land uses, together with policies which seek to set the parameters for how the intended development takes place. In the terminology adopted here the distinction between proposals and policies is that proposals relate to something which the local authority is promoting, and are site specific.

The approach which could be taken to these three components in undertaking an environmental appraisal can be described as follows.

Strategy

A strategy in a local plan should, from the environmental point of view:

- establish the overall approach of the plan towards the environment, and towards the balance of environmental with social and economic objectives
- set out a spatial strategy describing the characteristics of the relationship between land uses towards which the plan is aiming

The task of the appraisal is to identify whether the plan includes a strategy which sets appropriate environmental aims, and whether these aims are followed through in the subsequent proposals and policies in the plan. The strategy is not itself policy, and will not be a determining factor when development proposals are considered, so the aims have to be carried through in the expression of the policies. It is a simple and worthwhile exercise to see whether this is done, by linking individual policies to the stated aims of the strategy. If an aim has a proper planning purpose but this is not carried forward into any policy then this should be rectified.

The second requirement of the strategy encompasses the consideration of transport issues. The essential contribution of land use planning to the reduction of the impacts of transport - including the use of resources and the emission of CO_2 and other pollutants - will by influencing the inter-relationship of land uses, density, and ultimately the form of settlements. This cannot be done adequately at the time of individual proposals, but must be done when the development needs for some future period is under consideration, that is in the development plan.

The transport implications of different forms of development are not capable of being fully predicted, so that plan strategies should follow what is currently believed to be good practice.

Policies

Two questions are to be asked of the policies, defined for the present purpose in the terms above. These questions are:

- do the policies cover all of the environmental issues which it is appropriate for a land use plan to address, and are relevant to the local circumstances in the plan area?

38

- will the wording of the policy be effective in use?

Appraisal of the plan policies according to these question is a different exercise to the use of impact appraisal that is envisaged in the Guide, where the identification of impacts upon environmental stock is central. Experience has demonstrated that for those plan policies constructed specifically and explicitly to provide protection for a given element of environmental stock - agricultural land for instance - then undertaking an appraisal against a checklist of environmental stock is relatively uninformative. A policy which states that 'development which adversely affects (a given aspect of the environment) will be resisted' is single dimensional. It would be identified as having 'positive' impact upon the environmental element addressed by the policy, but be neutral in its impact upon all other aspects of the environment.

The impact of the policy is in any case a difficult idea since it is the way the policy influences development proposals that will be significant, and this will most often be a consequence of the integration of, and balancing between, many different policies and other considerations.

The level of insight provided by undertaking an impact appraisal for these types of policies is low. The more useful task is to ensure that all of the environmental issues which should be addressed in the plan are addressed. This is the exercise of 'scoping' referred to in the Good Practice Guide, and is undertaken in the environmental appraisal of the Consultation Draft of Northavon Local Plan for instance.

In the case of Narthavon the scoping lists - the checklists against which the plan can be checked - were produced by reference to current Government planning policy in the form of the Planning Policy Guidance Notes, the Minerals Planning Policy Guidance Notes and the Regional Planning Policy Guidance Notes. The number and range of issues on which the plan should include policies is usually found by this exercise to be wider than first appreciated.

Scoping against the content of the policy guidance may be less necessary as the familiarity with the newer wider environmental agenda increases. The content of development plans in future is more likely to be derived from and appraised by reference to performance indicators which describe the changes occurring or sought in the state of the environment, and which are capable of influence through land use planning.

Whilst plans should be consistent with national and regional policy guidance there are other 'unofficial' sources of assistance on the policy content of development plans. National bodies with an environmental role, statutory and non-statutory, have increasingly recognised the importance of influencing development plans in order to meet their objectives. Documents produced by such as the Countryside Commission (1993) and English Nature (1992b) are therefore valuable sources of advice on their respective topic areas. The CPRE as well as publishing high quality material intended to promote its own viewpoint has prepared useful reference lists to the source of environmental policy (CPRE 1994 a and b). The NRA and Friends of the Earth have both prepared material dealing specifically with the content of development plans, with the FoE's work a very useful exercise in translating the ideas of sustainability into practical material for inclusion in development plans on a topic by topic basis (FoE 1994).

Some environmental groups or NGOs have taken particular interest in the environmental appraisal of development plans. The work of the RSPB is valuable for instance with its general exploration of strategic environmental assessment and (RSPB 1993, 1994) and more recently has produced, with Bedfordshire County Council, a valuable complement to the DoE's Guide on environmental appraisal (Bedfordshire County Council 1996).

Consultation is an important part of producing development plans and the Guidelines emphasise the value in undertaking an environmental appraisal of involving those with expert environmental knowledge of the plan area. This may be representative of national bodies but it is also likely to be bodies such as the county wildlife trusts with a familiarity that the planning department is unlikely to ever attain.

Another useful sources of information and advice on the environmental content of development plans available to local planning authorities should be the work of other local planning authorities. This material would be particularly informative where a plan has been the subject of an Examination in Public or Public Local Inquiry and the Panel or Inspector's report provided some discussion of the merits of the approach taken. Policies included in approved or adopted plans can be used by others, in appropriate circumstances, with some confidence. Unfortunately however at the present time there is no comprehensive or readily accessible source of information about what other plans contain, or any central source of documents. Authorities have only their contact with neighbouring councils, and the valuable but hit and miss communication of journals and conferences to rely upon for the dissemination of best practice.

With the right set of issues addressed by policies then the effectiveness of the proposed policy is a matter for the appraisal. The concern for environmental appraisal is not with the plan itself, but with its consequences. The appraisal therefore should be interested in whether the policy will achieve its intended purpose in implementation. There is much in this type of practical approach to appraisal that overlaps with consideration of the plan from the point of view of development control. Several points can be made:

- it is a requirement of any policy that its meaning be clear, so it provides the user of the plan with an understanding of how a given development proposal might come to be considered; this is as true of environmental policies as of any others
- to achieve this clarity, and to be useful, each policy should deal with just one issue, and demonstrate how the implications of a proposal would be assessed in reaching a decision by the use of criteria

- attaching the same apparent degree of resistance to development when seeking the protection of different qualities of the same environmental feature creates an unclear situation and may dilute the protection provided in practice; the hierarchy inherent in the designation of landscape or nature conservation sites for instance should be reflected in the policies dealing with those designations
- the same point applies on a wider basis - a plan which simply lists every environmental feature as a reason to resist development but does not acknowledge the types of trade off inherent in meeting development needs, as it must itself provide for, is misleading and lays itself open to easy criticism
- policies expressed in terms such as 'to encourage' appear of little value; how is the Council to 'encourage' the achievement of the objective to which the plan aspires, and can a developer take policy support from a policy encouraging the recycling of land for a development proposal on disused land that is otherwise contrary to the plans aspirations for that land?

The general tightening of policies with an environmental purpose is good practice in appraisal, refining the policies so that they are more effective. Again 'best practice' is not coming into general use quickly enough in this area.

Proposals

The most significant, and most contested, part of a development plan is the identification of land for development. The proposed use of open land is opposed by those who would wish it to retain open and by those who would prefer land in which they have an interest to be used instead. The choice of sites for allocation in the plan is crucial to the overall environmental affect of the plan. The contribution of appraisal therefore is in assisting with the selection process and helping in the justification of the choices made.

For the proposals, environmental appraisal is very much an integral part of the plan's formulation rather than a check on the plan as a product. It is used in two stages:

- in making a choice
- in refining the proposals

There are potentially other roles too. Environmental appraisal could have a significant part to play in the determination of environmental capacity, if this concept becomes important in the development plan process, as it appears set to do. The Regional Guidance for the West Midlands already includes the statement: 'Development plans should ensure that the capacities of existing urban areas are maximised in as far as is consistent with securing quality of living environment' (DoE 1995, para.3.8)

Environmental capacity considerations would appear in the development planning

41

Global sustainability	Natural resources	Local environmental quality
Transport trips	Wildlife	Landscape and open land
Transport modes	Air quality	Cultural heritage
Built environment - energy efficiency	Water conservation and quality	Liveability Land and soil
Renewable energy	Land and soil	Open space
CO_2 fixing	Minerals conservation	Building quality

Figure 3.1 Environmental stock

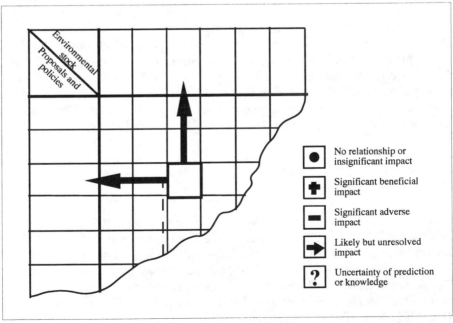

Figure 3.2 An impact appraisal matrix

process at the state of determining the overall quantum of development rather than its location, and probably when strategically set targets were being challenged.

The best way of examining the impact of possible development proposals at the development plan stage is by the form of impact appraisal suggested in the Good Practice Guide. The first step is to identify a number of factors which 'describe' the environment in a comprehensive yet manageable way. This is the 'environmental stock'. Figure 3.1 presents a typical list of distinctive environmental issues or elements that is intended to be a comprehensive yet manageable and which can be used to characterise' the environment upon which the plan might have an impact.

The second step is to consider whether the consequences of implementing the proposal would be harmful or beneficial - that is negative or positive.

The usual way to present the results of this impact appraisal is in the form of matrices. Figure 3.2 illustrates the use of a matrix and explains a set of symbols which can be used in the process. The use of matrices has a number of advantages:

- it organises the undertaking of the appraisal, ensuring that all of the possible impacts are considered for all of the proposals in a systematic way.
- it provides a visual demonstration that this has been done.
- by scanning the matrix the proposals which have high numbers of either positive or negative impacts are readily identifiable.

The Guide does not recommend that numerical systems be used, either to 'weight' the relative importance of the environmental issues, or to 'score' the significance of the identified impacts. There is no common base for the comparison of the environmental stock under consideration and the attribution and summation of scores is a false exercise. The decision process does not become more objective, it is merely that the assumptions and preferences are disguised behind an apparently scientific approach.

The decision process within development plans is different to that which would be implied were scores in the matrix added together. The reality is that the decision takers are choosing to favour one or more factors (environmental or otherwise) against others. Preparing impact appraisal matrices of options (ie before a choice is made) allows the decision taker to see which options are favoured if importance is attached to particular issues.

Whilst it is not felt appropriate to attach weighting to different aspects of the environmental stock, or to prescribe a strict hierarchy, most lists which have been developed by local authorities for their use, or recommended by environmental commentators do use some categorisation. This approach assists in organising the stock to produce a list which is comprehensive yet comprises distinctive items, and which is as short as possible. It also indicates an element of hierarchy, or at least requires acknowledgement that different types of issues are being traded. A frequently adopted division is to split the stock list into:

43

- global sustainability
- natural resource management
- local environmental quality

The inclusion of 'local environmental quality' provides for local circumstances and perhaps particular concerns of the Council Members whilst ensuring that these issues are seen in context.

There are inevitable difficulties in definition and categorisation since whilst many aspects are clearly local and other clearly global (transcending the administrative area which is the subject of the plan for instance), others are less clear cut. Matters of nature conservation are difficult to 'place' in any categorisation.

Refinement

It is part of the task of development plans to identify land for development, to contribute to identified economic and social needs. The reality is therefore that the plan will have to countenance environmental impacts. There are more environmental issues now identified as a matter for concern and the opportunities to meet development needs with insignificant effects upon the environment are diminishing. Part of the task is to inform the choice over which environmental matters are affected - acknowledging matters hitherto ignored perhaps - and part of the task in appraisal is to oblige a robust justification to be provided. But the additional value of appraisal is its potential for improving a proposal through refinement. Improvement here means reducing the harmful impacts upon the environment whilst still meeting the social and economic objectives.

In the event of a draft proposal being found through impact appraisal to be likely to have impacts, Figure 3.3 shows the possible responses. The value of appraisal is that it indicates the type of change to a proposal that will improve the overall environmental performance of the plan.

Figure 3.4 takes a specific type of development proposal - a business park on peripheral urban site - to show how it might be improved through refinement.

Comments on the use of environmental appraisal

The limitations of environmental appraisal as a process of informing choice are primarily those of knowledge and understanding. We do not know enough about, for instance, how the disposition of employment opportunities in relation to housing locations can change patterns of travel, and hence change the use of energy and the emissions of pollutants.

Neither do we have a really objective basis for deciding that one type of impact is better than another. How is the introduction of a higher resident population into the vicinity of an historic woodland to be compared with building near or over an

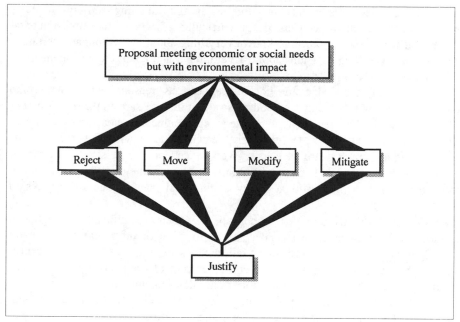

Figure 3.3   Refinement of a proposal with negative environmental impact

Example	Proposal to establish a peripheral employment site
Principle	Negative impact Conflict with principles of sustainable development at global and local level
Detail	Some positive impact Contribution to landscape enhancement and conservation objectives
Justification	Strategic requirement for employment sites to diversify economy through inward investment
Review	Can economic requirement be met whilst reducing negative impacts? For example - density controls - reduced car parking standard - limited range of uses - genuine 'new industry' rather than out of centre locations - increased contribution - eg community forest

Figure 3.4   Specific example of proposal refinement

aquifer? Knowledge is advancing, and so is the lobbying activity of those knowledgeable about or concerned for particular aspects of the environmental stock. But we can never expect to know everything about everything and certainly cannot put off making decisions about development and about the management of the environment until we do.

The limits of knowledge are not to be seen as reasons not to undertake environmental appraisal, but are good reason why it necessary in the development planning process. Not being able to define an environmental impact does not mean that impact will not occur. Development decisions taken without some form of environmental appraisal are in effect given precedence to those environmental issues which are known, familiar and relatively predictable over those which are more difficult, or which national policy or the local planning authority seeks to avoid.

An example is easily provided. Landscape has been a significant and regularly used environmental issue in considering the location of development for many years, but issues such as nature conservation and water quality only more recently so. Where it exists (and it does so over 12 per cent of England). Green Belt has probably been the single most important determinant of the location of development. Yet Green Belt policy and Green Belt designation takes no account of the implications for transport of development locations.

Environmental appraisal does not claim to provide an entirely rational means of making planning decisions, since there can be no such thing. What it is is an attempt to ensure that the full range of environmental issues are taken into account when policies and proposals are formulated in a development plan, and that it is demonstrated how those environmental matters have been taken into account.

Identifying impacts in this way does not remove from the decision taker the task of arriving at a choice, but it does assist in informing that choice. Environmental appraisal in development plans, coupled with the requirement for full coverage by development plans, is a move towards a rational, consistent and open approach to decision making in planning. It points too to the need to make difficult decisions, if planning's traditional concern for the 'public interest' is to embrace the future as well as the present.

There are other forces in planning. Politicians at the national and local level are showing little enthusiasm for the difficult decisions demanded by a shift towards greater sustainability when these come to be made. The absence of any serious attempt to bring about the more appropriate use of motor cars is the obvious example. In matters of development any move towards the adoption of rational decision processes poses a serious constraint upon political flexibility. Current concerns about the emergence and operation of this round of development plans may bring down the plan-led system, or more positively may hasten the evolution of an approach which more accurately reflects the nature of the decision process when good planning prevails. If this is the route which planning follows, then environmental appraisal will have been formative in its emergence and essential to its operation.

These are still early days for environmental appraisal and interesting times for planning. If environmental appraisal prospers it will lead to better development plans, better planning decisions, and better management of the environment.

Notes

1 Section 54A Town and Country Planning Act 1990; and see PPG1: General Principles (DoE 1992 a)

References

Baker, J. (1995), 'Turbulent ride ahead for strategic sustainability' *Planning No. 1123*, Ambit: Gloucester.

Bedfordshire County Council and Royal Society for the Protection of Birds (1996), *A Step by Step Guide to Environmental Appraisal*, Bedfordshire County Council: Bedford.

Countryside Commission, English Heritage, English Nature (1993), *Conservation Issues in Strategic Plans*, CCP420, Countryside Commission: Northampton.

Council for the Protection of Rural England (1994a), *Environmental Policy Omissions in Development Plans*, CPRE: London.

Council for the Protection of Rural England (1994b), *Greening the Regions*, CPRE: London.

Department of the Environment (1991), *Policy Appraisal and the Environment. A Guide for Government Departments*, HMSO: London

Department of the Environment (1992a), *Planning Policy Guidance 1 General Policy and Principles*, HMSO: London.

Department of the Environment (1992b), *Planning Policy Guidance 12 Development Plans and Regional Planning Guidance*, HMSO: London.

Department of the Environment (1993), *The Environmental Appraisal of Development Plans: A Good Practice Guide*, HMSO: London.

Department of the Environment (1995), *Regional planning Guidance for the West Midlands RPG11*, HMSO: London.

English Nature (1992), *Strategic Planning and Sustainable Development: An Informal Consultation Paper*, English Nature: Peterborough.

Friends of the Earth (1994), *Planning for the planet: sustainable development policies for local and strategic plans*, FoE: London.

Hinkley and Bosworth Borough Council (1995), *Environmental Appraisal of Hinkley and Bosworth Local Plan*, Hinkley and Bosworth Local Plan: Hinkley.

Kent County Council (1993), *Strategic Environmental Assessment of Policies: Working paper No. 193 to Kent Structure Plan*, Kent County Council: Maidstone.

Lancashire County Council (1993), *Strategic Environmental Appraisal of the 1986-1996 Lancashire Structure Plan: Technical Report No. 13*, Lancashire County Council: Preston.

Mendip District Council (1995), *Mendip District Local Plan Consultation Paper*, Mendip District Council: Shepton Mallet

Mendip District Council (1996), *Strategic Analysis of SpatiaL Patterns in the Mendip District*, Mendip District Council: Shepton Mallet

Mole Valley District Council (1996) *Mole Valley Local Plan Deposit Version*, Mole Valley District Council: Dorking.

Northavon District Council (1994), *Northavon Local Plan Consultation Draft*, South Gloucestershire Council: Thornbury.

Royal Society for the Protection of Birds (1993), *The new age of environmental policy - delivering sustainable land use in the 1990s*, RSPB: Sandy.

Royal Society for the Protection of Birds (1994), *Environmental challenge 1994: an agenda for local government*, RSPB: Sandy.

Therivel, R. (1994) 'Environmental appraisal of development plans in practice' *Built Environment*, Vol. 20, No. 4, pp.45-48.

U.K. Government (1990), *This Common Inheritance*, CM1200, HMSO: London

4 Sustainability indicators: a new tool for evaluation?

Graham Pinfield

Introduction

Over the past few years the concept of sustainable development has become the guiding principle for environmental policy in an increasing number of organisations from a local to an international level. Whilst the definition, objectives and practical implications of the concept are still subject of much debate, some of the most interesting discussions and initiatives have been about the key information sets or 'indicators' needed to define policy and measure progress. A proliferation of initiatives world-wide is seeking to address this issue and 'sustainability indicators' are seen increasingly as tools to help policy makers crystallise issues, identify policy responses and monitor progress towards goals and targets. (See for example Pinfield 1993; LGMB et al. 1994; MacGillivray and Zadek 1995; and Pinter 1995)

Indicators, however, are not only a tool for policy makers. They can also help set new political agendas and encourage community interest and involvement in sustainable development. Indeed many of the most well-known indicator exercises, for example those of Seattle (Sustainable Seattle 1995) and Jacksonville (Jacksonville Community Council Inc. 1993) in the United States have been participatory processes aimed at creating new goals for local politicians and policy makers based on community perceptions of what is important. This chapter outlines the role of indicators in formulating policies for sustainable development. It looks first at the need and justification for sustainability indicators arising out of Agenda 21 and other documents. It then gives a brief review of activity in this field from an international to a local level. The chapter goes on to examine how indicators are being used to appraise policies and projects and used to ensure that these contribute towards sustainability. The chapter concludes by examining the use of indicators to encourage public participation in sustainability initiatives.

The need for sustainability indicators

The Brundtland Commission (World Commission on Environment and Development 1987) firmly established the concept of sustainable development as one that integrated economic, social and environmental policy in order to:

> make development sustainable to ensure that it meets the needs of the present without compromising the ability of future generations to meet their own needs. (WCED 1987, p.43)

Caring for the Earth (IUCN, WWF, UNEP, 1991) redefined sustainable development as:

> Improving the quality of life while living within the carrying capacity of supporting ecosystems (IUCN, WWF, UNEP 1991, p.10).

Both definitions imply concern for the long term health and integrity of the environment, for meeting needs and adding to quality of life of current generations, and for the needs of future generations also to be considered.

In order to bring into balance the economic, social and environmental dimensions of human activity, information is required on the on key aspects of each of these systems. Chapter 40 of Agenda 21 (UNCED 1992) calls for countries to develop indicators of sustainable development and use them to develop policy, informed by better and more systematic information about environmental, economic and social factors. It also calls for information to be better co-ordinated and transformed into forms useful for decision-taking. However, little detail is given on how this is to be achieved and which agencies are likely to play a role, and there is clear concern that current information and information systems are not adequate to guide policy and action for sustainable development.

The sustainable development scenario is often depicted as in Figure 4.1 with sustainable development at the interface between policies for economic development, community development and ecological development. Sustainable development is seen to be development that is people-centred, seeking to improve the human condition, and environment-centred, seeking to sustain the variety and productivity of the earth. Sustainable development would, in theory, bring the three spheres into closer and closer union until economic development is contained within environmental and societal limits and the needs of the population are met over the long term and into the next generation. However, economic growth (rather than welfare) currently dominates policy-making in governments of the industrialised world and many authors (see, for example, Douthwaite 1992; and Hoogendijk 1993) have argued that rather than benefiting the population or the planet as a whole such policies have, over the past few decades, only served to perpetuate inequalities and threaten the environment. Hoogendijk has likened the economies of modern countries to 'giants off-balance' which are compelled to run

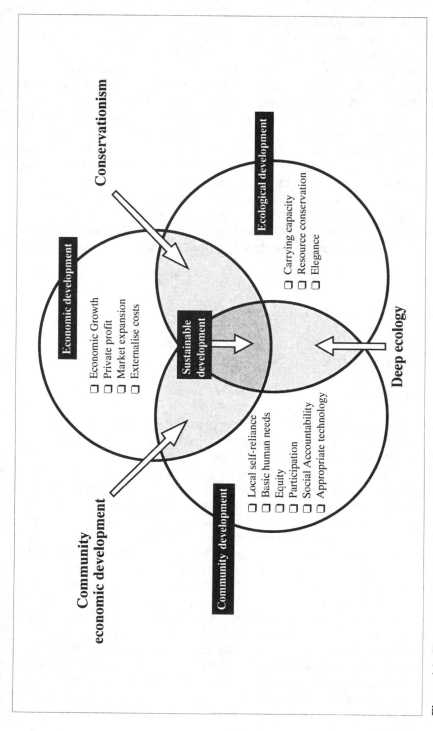

Figure 4.1 The sustainable development challenge
Source : International Council for Local Environmental Initiatives (1995)

51

(or grow) in order not to fall. Hoogendijk sees the compulsion for growth as being formed by numerous cultural and institutional forces including the money system itself. Sustainability meanwhile will require 'a severe cut in today's production volumes and a basic change in the nature of production' (Hoogendijk 1993, p.17).

The Commission for Sustainable Development (CSD), which was set up in June 1993, is charged with monitoring progress on implementation of Agenda 21. The CSD has taken an increasing interest in indicators as a way of monitoring the progress being made by national governments in implementing commitments to sustainable development. National reports submitted to the Commission to date have, however, been poor in terms of precise information on trends and how these should be monitored over time. Organisations such as the World Wide Fund for Nature and New Economics Foundation have consequently been pressing the Commission to identify indicators that could be used to monitor national performance (NEF and WWF 1994). The Commission is now beginning to define a clear role for indicators as a foundation for decision-making about sustainable development.

Sustainability indicator initiatives - a brief review

It is important to have indicators of sustainability so that trends can be established and targets for improvement can be set. This is what many sustainability indicator exercises seek to achieve.

The most widely used indicator of progress in society is the gross national product (GNP) which measures the total output of goods and services in the economy. GNP is used to rank countries as rich or poor and 'developed' or 'developing'. A rising GNP (economic growth) is often presumed to show that a country's economy is improving and its people becoming 'better off'. If the GNP is declining then the country is said to be going into recession. This way of assessing progress has become institutionalised across the globe in the system of National Income Accounts which were agreed by the United Nations in 1968. GNP as a measure, however, has many shortcomings, for example, it includes expenditure that damages the environment (the depletion of natural resources and so-called 'defensive expenditures') but completely ignores essential (but un-paid) activity in the home or voluntary activity of benefit to local communities.

Growing realisation of the failings of GNP has spurred numerous attempts to either devise ways of adjusting the national accounts or to devise completely different sets of indicators of progress. The United Nations Development Programme's Human Development Index (UNDP 1990) was an early attempt to present three alternative indicators, longevity, literacy and purchasing power, into a single index. Daly and Cobbs' Index of Sustainable Economic Welfare (ISEW) combined ecological factors with statistics on income distribution, capital growth, value of household labour, and public expenditures on health and education. This work has illustrated how, over the past 20 years, human welfare has declined while

GNP has continued to rise (Daly and Cobb 1990).

A more recent approach, and one that characterises the sustainability indicators movement, is to present an array of indicators measuring progress on a number of fronts. With this approach no attempt is made to aggregate the indicators into a single index or relate them in any way to GNP or to other national (economic) indicators. Seen collectively, sustainability indicators are intended to measure progress on how well society is advancing towards its sustainability goals.

Many of the more recent attempts to devise sustainability indicators are locally initiated and co-ordinated and attempt to capture important aspects of local life, culture or environment . One of the most well-known of these is the Sustainable Seattle Indicators Programme which began in 1992. The aims of this project, backed by a number of different sectoral groups, is to collect, agree upon and publicise a set of indicators of sustainability in order to make them accessible to the public and to decision-makers . A similar exercise has been conducted since 1985 in Jacksonville, Florida, where 'Life in Jacksonville: Quality Indicators for Progress' tracks the trends in quality of life indicators identified through a process of community consultation. This involved citizen task forces, opinion surveys and community meetings co-ordinated by the Jacksonville Community Council.

Following on from the type of approach adopted in Seattle and Jacksonville, but linked to the post-Rio emphasis on Local Agenda 21 and 'bottom-up' change, is the UK's Sustainability Indicators Research Project. This has involved the Local Government Management Board, the Local Authority Associations and ten local authorities since 1993 in a project which has sought to identify a set of indicators for use in local sustainable development policy and planning (LGMB 1994, 1995a, 1995b, 1995c).

The approach taken in this project has been to develop a framework for indicator development based on the UNEP definition of sustainable development (see above). The two key elements of sustainability - improving 'quality of life' within the 'carrying capacity' of the earth - were taken as broad categories under which a more detailed set of goals could be defined. These goals, identified as those for a sustainable community, are shown in Table 4.1.

Each of these goals was used to define a specific set of indicators which would measure progress towards the objective. Over one hundred indicators, many derived from other similar studies carried out elsewhere, were allocated under each of the themes. This menu of goals and indicators was then taken by each of the pilot authorities for six months of rigorous 'road testing' with local communities. This menu proved useful in many of the pilot areas but there was a clear and understandable desire by the pilot communities to highlight local issues and reflect local circumstances. These helped to shape the indicators that were chosen by each local authority. As a guide a number of criteria for selecting indicators were given. The most important of these were that indicators should (LGMB 1995c, p.16):

- be significant in terms of sustainability

53

- have a clear and reasoned bearing on sustainability at both global and local levels
- be relevant both to ordinary citizens and policy-makers
- reflect local circumstances
- be based on information which can be collected
- show trends over a reasonable timescale
- have a relationship to other indicators
- be meaningful both individually and collectively
- be clear and easy to understand
- provoke change (eg. in policies, services or lifestyles)
- lead to the setting of targets or thresholds

Table 4.1 The main themes of sustainable development

A sustainable community would be one in which:
- resources are used efficiently, waste is minimised and materials are recycled;
- pollution is limited to levels which do not cause damage to natural ecosystems;
- the diversity of nature is valued and protected;
- where possible, local needs are met locally;
- everyone has access to adequate food, water, shelter and fuel at a reasonable cost;
- everyone has the opportunity to undertake satisfying work in a diverse economy. The value of unpaid work is recognised, and payment for work is both fair and fairly distributed;
- health is protected by the creation of safe, clean and pleasant environments and of services which emphasise prevention of illness as well as care for the sick;
- access to facilities, services, goods and other people is not achieved at the expense of the environment or limited to those with cars;
- people live without fear of crime, or persecution on account of their race, gender, sexuality or beliefs;
- everyone has access to the skills, knowledge and information which they need to play a full part in society;
- all sections of the community are empowered to participate in decision making;
- opportunities to participate in culture, leisure and recreation are readily available to all, and;
- buildings, open spaces and artifacts combine meaning with beauty and utility; settlements are 'human' in scale and form; and diversity and distinctive local features are valued and protected

Source: LGMB (1995c)

Not all the indicators from the original menu proved popular in the pilot exercise and those that were adopted were sometimes modified in the course of selection. A number of locally important indicators, for example, the incidence of child asthma in Merton; the occurrence of frogs and newts in ponds in Oldham; and the quality of Leicester city centre were just some that were developed by the pilot communities.

Several of the UK Sustainability Indicator Research Project authorities have now collected data for the various indicators that emerged from their piloting processes and have published reports presenting data on the various indicators (see for example, Oldham MBC (1995), London Borough of Merton (1995), Fife Regional Council (1995) and Strathclyde Regional Council (1995). These 'Sustainabilty Reports' present each indicator together with: (a) a brief discussion of the sustainability issue it relates to; (b) a definition of the indicator and a description of how it is measured; (c) an interpretation of the data including any discernable trends and relationship to targets; and (d) an assessment of how it is linked to other indicators (see the example of a Strathclyde indicator shown in Figure 4.2). Some pilots (for example, Oldham and Leicester) have also given ideas for action to achieve change in the indicator and who may be responsible for this. The recently published guide to Sustainability Reporting (LGMB 1996) provides further advice on how to carry out and collate information on local sustainabilty conditions.

Once in possession of this baseline information on sustainability conditions it is then a simple step to begin using the indicators and the goals to which they relate to appraise policies. Environmental appraisal is covered elsewhere in this book (see Chapter 3) and 'sustainability appraisal' is fundamentally similar except that it uses the broader range of indicators covered in the Sustainability Report as the baseline information against which to appraise impacts.

Sustainability indicators and policy evaluation

The idea of using sustainability indicators to appraise and evaluate existing policies and help in the formulation of new policies is a logical extension of work already carried out on environmental appraisal. Environmental appraisal uses as its starting point an understanding of local environmental conditions and then uses this information to predict the impact of various strategies, policies and policy options (DoE 1993). Sustainability appraisal uses the information gathered and published in the sustainability report to carry out a systematic assessment of the sustainability impact of proposed policies. Despite the apparent obviousness of this approach few of the UK Sustainability pilots have yet undertaken such appraisals.

'Environ', the environmental charity based in Leicester, have produced a 'sustainability checklist' for City council officers to appraise projects and policies (Roberts et al 1996). The checklist consists of forty criteria phrased as questions grouped under eight headings (Transport; Economy and Work; Pollution; Community and Participation; Energy; Waste and Resources; Wildlife and Open

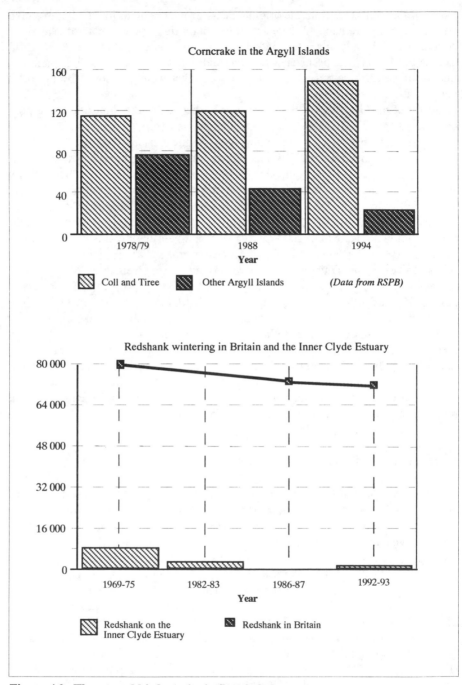

Figure 4.2 Threatened bird species in Strathclyde
Source : Strathclyde Regional Council (1995)

Spaces; and Buildings and Land Use). Officers are asked to complete an appraisal form for each proposal scoring the project or policy as positive, negative or neutral against each of the specified criteria. It is suggested that an overall 'sustainability score' can then be calculated by totting up the total number of positive over negative scores. The form also contains room for notes and comments on how improvements could be made to the proposal, or to flag up any particularly strong impacts on any aspect of sustainability that may be lost in the overall score. One of the questions in each section relates to 'equity' or areas of greatest need, e.g. whether the proposal involves under-represented groups such as ethnic minorities or the disabled these are summed separately to give an 'equity score'. Environ consider that the value of the checklist is threefold. First, it helps councils appraise and therefore ensure that projects and policies contribute towards sustainability. Second, it allows officers to propose projects bearing in mind the points needed for sustainability. Thirdly, it demonstrates that sustainability is about the integration of social, economic and environmental factors. The projects that have multiple benefits on all these fronts will score highest on the checklist.

The Environ checklist is not drawn directly from the Sustainability Report 'Indicators of Sustainable Development in Leicester - Progress and Trends' (Jeffcote et al. 1995) but is similar to the approach adopted by the Environment Cities in the Environment City Index published in 'Stepping Stones'(Wood 1995). This used eight topics (Energy; Transport; Waste and Pollution; Food and Agriculture; Economy and Work; Built Environment; Natural Environment; and Social Environment) based on the Specialist Working Groups used in most Environment Cities, as a basis for a similar scoring exercise on projects. For each topic there are four levels of positive impact and four categories of negative impact. The resulting chart (see Figure 4.3) is intended to show the broad positive and negative impacts of any particular project.

The Regional Municipality Hamilton-Wentworth in Ontario, Canada has devised a 'Sustainable Community Decision-Making Guide' (Hamilton-Wentworth 1993) which sets out in a more comprehensive way a series of steps to be taken to appraise any council decisions for their impact on the overall social, environmental, and economic health of the community. The decision-making guide is tied to the wider goals for sustainability that the municipality has adopted in its 'Vision 2020' document (Hamilton-Wentworth 1994) and to a set of indicators (currently being defined) that will measure progress towards these goals.

The guide sets out a three stage process, each with its own series of steps and forms to prepare. The first part looks at problem identification, the second at assessment of solutions and the third part at recommendations. The recommended solutions are incorporated into committee reports to enable the Regional Council to make a decision about whether the proposal fits in with the overall direction of Vision 2020. In this way the decision-making guide (which uses an illustration of a stool balanced on three legs - economic, social and environmental - representing good decisions) fits into an overall framework for the management of sustainable development within the Council (see Figure 4.4).

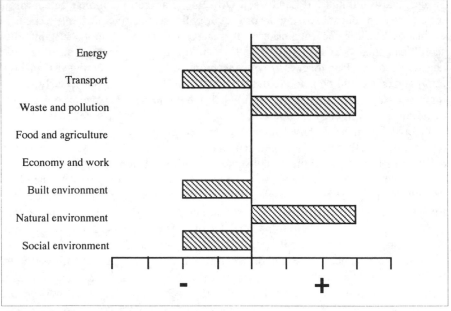

Figure 4.3 The environment city index
Source : Wood (1995)

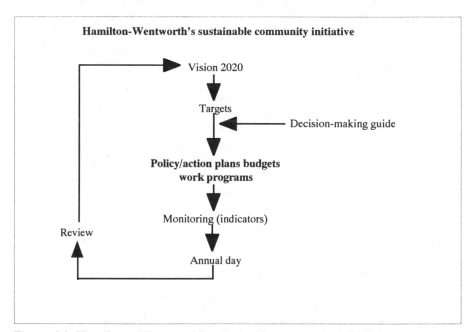

Figure 4.4 Hamilton - Wentworth's sustainable community initiative
Source : Hamilton - Wentworth (1994)

The decision-making guide plays an important role in ensuring that the Council's policies practices and spending are in line with sustainable development and the Vision 2020 goals.

The holistic and thorough approach to 'sustainability appraisal' adopted by Hamilton-Wentworth and suggested to an extent by Environ improves upon traditional environmental appraisal in two clear ways. First, environmental, social and economic objectives are considered together and 'balanced'by looking at the positive and negative impacts on each and considering these together thus helping to avoid 'trade off' situations. Secondly, in Hamilton-Wentworth these various objectives form part of an overall vision for sustainable development adopted by the Council and appraisal can therefore perform a positive role in guiding proposals towards corporately agreed objectives. This avoids the appraisal being seen as a negative and time consuming exercise seeking to constrain development proposals.

Sustainability indicators, policies and public participation

The process of policy-making for sustainable development as outlined in Agenda 21 requires a relationship between the institutions of government and the public. Agenda 21 recognised that community participation in decisions for sustainable development was vital because the outcomes would need to be widely supported, not least because many of the policy shifts required would be so radical that politicians would want to be assured of public support. Further, people would also need to make their own contribution by living more sustainable lifestyles. If 'development' is seen to be more than just economic growth but about meeting people's needs and aspirations to develop in a variety of social, cultural and environmental ways, then the community would have to be involved in identifying and formulating values and priorities.

The role for sustainability indicators as perceived in the UK Sustainability Indicators Project, and in other similar exercises such as Seattle, is in identifying and quantifying current sustainability conditions and to point the way towards more sustainable conditions. Through a process led by government (national and local) and business, with the involvement and support of the public, it is anticipated that indicators can help moves towards a more sustainable situation (depicted in the lower part of the Figure 4.5) where a state of sustainability is reached (Macnaghten et al. 1995). Many sustainability indicator exercises attempt to carry out this role. Some, like those of the UK Sustainability Indicator pilots, highlight unwelcome social trends (such as rises in homelessness, crime, and poverty) and many trends towards sustainability (for example, improvements in river water quality). Seattle use pointing arrows to show trends towards or away from sustainability and this technique has been adopted by many of the UK pilots (LGMB 1995b).

The problem for many indicator exercises lies in the assumption shown in the middle part of the diagram that relies on the existence of a relationship between the

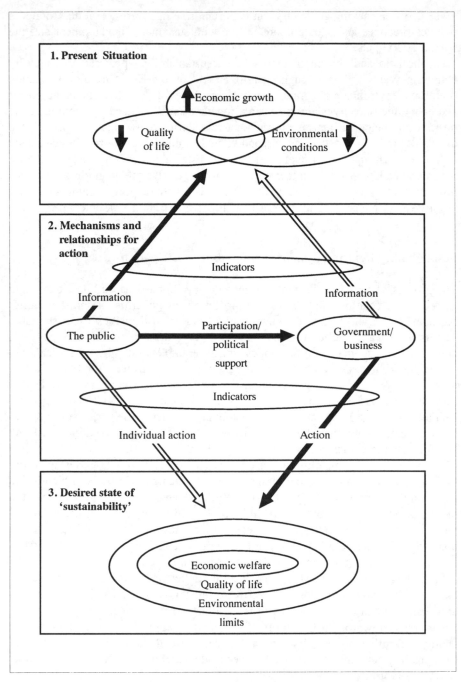

Figure 4.5   Model of sustainability and the role envisaged for indicators
Source : Macnaghten et al (1995)

public and representative institutions. Several studies (see, for example, Macnaghten et al. 1995; Jowell et al. 1995) have shown that the relationship of trust between the public and political institutions, particularly in the UK, has broken down. These institutions are seen increasingly to be unlistening, out-of-touch with people's concerns and needs, and instead are seen to serve their own bureaucratic interests. These findings have profound implications for the effectiveness of indicators as a tool to encourage community participation in (predominantly) government-led initiatives for sustainable development.

It is becoming increasingly clear that if indicators are to be truly effective then there needs to be some constitutional change brought about in parallel. Along these lines MacGillivray and Zadek (1995, p.3) have argued for:

> a radical shake-up in the way in which key decisions are made. In effect .... a reconstitution of the governance of, and operational framework for, many of today's international, and national institutions including their relationship with other parts of civil society.

Local government, which plays such a crucial part in implementing Agenda 21 at the local level, needs to change radically its own relationship with its local communities. Sadly, few UK local authorities are making any significant new steps to develop a closer and more empowering relationship with their citizens.

Linked to the institutional change required are changes in attitudes and perceptions by policy-makers within government. There are still the belief within some organisations that the identification of precise levels of pollutants and thresholds by experts is seen as the best way to bring about change in public attitudes and behaviour. If the public are to be engaged in action on sustainability then the development of policy needs to be more an exercise in information, negotiation, deliberation and consensus-building with the population than it is at present. Views of local people about the issues and indicators that affect and reflect their lives and experiences will need to be sought and then co-operative ways to tackle the issues agreed upon. This process will then rely upon a relationship of trust between each of the partners to implement their part of the solution that will, in turn, influence the trend in the particular indicator.

Whilst the process of generating indicators is certainly important, and was one of the key benefits identified by the UK Sustainability Indicators Project pilots, it is obviously important that indicators should be translated into policy and action. Though it is still early days there is little evidence, even amongst those pioneering local authorities mentioned here, that sustainability indicators are bringing about the radical shifts in policy that Hoogendijk and many other commentators have called for. It is perhaps necessary that there should be an incremental process of change and it is obvious that change will be reliant upon a number of contextual elements being in place. For example, in order for indicators to make any headway there is a need to change political attitudes and priorities, away from the promotion of economic growth as a primary aim for government policy towards general social and environmental well-being (and indicators themselves can help bring this about). Linked to this there will also be a need to change the culture and operation of political institutions along the lines described above. Governmental (national and local) policy-making needs to be far more transparent and open to influence by the general public with whom a relationship of trust needs to be re-established. In many cases there will be a need for education and awareness-raising amongst the population at large in order for the full implications and issues of sustainable development to be fully grasped and acted upon.

Summary

This chapter has demonstrated the growing importance of sustainability indicators in establishing a basis for policy and measuring progress towards sustainable development. It is a role seen as critical by the Commission for Sustainable Development in monitoring progress made by national governments towards goals agreed in Agenda 21.

Many indicator exercises have been spawned because of a growing realisation of the inadequacies of Gross National Product as a measure of human welfare. However, various attempts to highlight and make adjustments to GNP, for example, the Index for Sustainable Economic Welfare, whilst highlighting the shortcomings have failed to make any fundamental impact on the use of GNP as an overall measure of progress.

A more recent trend has been to develop local sustainability indicators either by community-based organisations or by local authorities in partnership with local communities. Such exercises have concentrated on developing locally-derived and important indicators of progress which are intended to influence local governmental policies through a process of bottom-up change. The chapter has highlighted some examples where sustainability indicators are being used for policy appraisal and has shown how this can be a positive way to evaluate the impact of policies and ensure their consistency with sustainability objectives.

However, the permeation of sustainability into mainstream political policy-making remains very small. Several factors may be inhibiting or delaying this process. In parallel with the development of indicators there is a need to bring about a change in political priorities, a change in the culture and operation of political institutions and for a new relationship of trust and understanding to be developed between these institutions and the population around new goals for society, the environment and the economy.

References

Daly, H and Cobb, J. (1990), *For the Common Good*, Beacon Press: Boston.

Department of the Environment (1993), *Environmental Appraisal of Development Plans - A Good Practice Guide.* HMSO: London.

Douthwaite, R . (1992), *The Growth Illusion*, Green Books: Bideford

Fife Regional Council (1995), *Sustainability Indicators for Fife,* Fife Regional Council: Glenrothes

Hamilton-Wentworth (1993), *Sustainable Community Decision-Making Guide*, Regional Municipality of Hamilton Wentworth: Ontario.

Hamilton-Wentworth (1994), *Vision 2020* , Regional Municipality of Hamilton-Wentworth: Ontario.

Hoogendijk, W. (1993), *The Economic Revolution*, International Books: Utrecht.

International Council for Local Environmental Initiatives (1995), *Local Agenda 21 Planning Guide (Draft)*, ICLEI: Toronto.

IUCN (World Conservation Union); World Wide Fund for Nature; United Nations Environment Programme (1991), *Caring for the Earth*, Earthscan: London.

Jacksonville Community Council Inc. (1993), *Life in Jacksonville. Quality Indicators for Progress*, Jacksonville Community Council Inc. : Florida.

Jeffcote, M., Allen, M., Newby, L. (1995), *Indicators of Sustainable Development in Leicester - Progress and Trends*, Environ/Leicester City Council: Leicester.

Jowell,R., Curtice, J., Park, A.,Brook, L., and Ahrendt, D. (eds) (1995), *British Social Attitudes the 12th Report*, Social and Community Planning Research: Aldershot.

Local Government Management Board (1994), *The Sustainability Indicators Research Project; Report of Phase One*, LGMB: Luton.

Local Government Management Board (1995a), *The Sustainability Indicators Research Project; Guidance to Pilot Authorities*, LGMB: Luton.

Local Government Management Board (1995b), *The Sustainability Indicators Research Project; Report of Phase Two*, LGMB: Luton.

Local Government Management Board (1995c), *The Sustainability Indicators Research Project; Indicators for Local Agenda 21 - A Summary*, LGMB: Luton.

Local Government Management Board (1996), *Local Authority Sustainability Auditing - A Guide for UK Local Authorities*, LGMB: Luton.

London Borough of Merton (1995), *Indicators for a Sustainable Future*, Merton Local Advisory Group: Merton.

Macnaghten, P., Grove-White, R., Jacobs, M. and Wynne, B. (1995), *Public Perceptions and Sustainability in Lancashire : Indicators, Institutions, Participation*, Lancashire County Council: Preston.

MacGillivray, A., and Zadek, S. (1995), *Accounting for Change: An Essential Guide to Sustainable Development Indicators*, New Economics Foundation: London.

New Economics Foundation and World Wide Fund for Nature (1994), *Indicators for Action : Commission on Sustainable Development*, NEF / WWF: London.

Oldham Metropolitan Borough Council (1995), *Sustainability Indicators for Oldham*, Oldham MBC: Oldham.

Pinfield, G. (1993), *Indicators for Sustainable Development*, Unpublished MSc thesis. Liverpool John Moores University: Liverpool.

Pinter, L . (1995), *Performance Measurement for Sustainable Development : Compendium of Experts, Initiatives and Publications*, International Institute for Sustainable Development: Canada.

Roberts,I., Newby,L., and Bell,D., *et al* (1996), *Local Sustainability*, Environ: Leicester.

Strathclyde Regional Council (1995), *Strathclyde Sustainability Indicators*, Strathclyde Regional Council: Glasgow.

Sustainable Seattle (1995), *Indicators of Sustainable Community 1995*, Sustainable Seattle: Seattle.

United Nations Commission on Environment and Development (UNCED) (1992), *Agenda 21*, UNCED: New York.

United Nations Development Programme (1990), *Human Development Report 1990 and 1991*. Oxford University Press: Oxford.

Whittaker, S. (1995), *First Steps - Local Agenda 21 in Practice*, HMSO: London.

Wood, C. (1995), *Stepping Stones II - The Inside Story,* The Wildlife Trusts/BT Environment City: Lincoln.

World Commission on Environment and Development (1987), *Our Common Future*, Oxford University Press: Oxford.

5 Environmental targets in land-use planning

Dominic Stead

> Targets can give policy a clearer sense of direction; they can add to the pace of policy implementation and development; and they can make explicit those aspects of policy that might otherwise remain opaque (House of Lords Select Committee on Sustainable Development, 1995, p.16)

Environmental targets are relatively new policy tools and have recently found an important role in the policy-implementation process, particularly since incorporation of the concept of sustainable development into policy making. Environmental targets are being increasingly advocated as a tool for more sustainable land-use planning (e.g. EU Expert Group on the Urban Environment 1994; Jacobs 1993; McLaren and Bosworth 1994; English Nature 1994), and are already being used in other countries (e.g. The Netherlands) as a basis for policy making. The House of Lords inquiry into the UK sustainable development strategy has recently called for the process of setting targets to be broadened and quickened (House of Lords 1995, p.73). The future role of environmental targets in policy may therefore become increasingly important.

This chapter examines the current and future potential roles of environmental targets in the policy-implementation process, and how they can contribute to more sustainable land-use planning. The chapter begins by tracing some of the reasons behind the current interest in environmental targets and examines the role of environmental targets in the policy-implementation process. The process of target setting is then examined, and examples of environmental targets in land-use planning policy identified. Finally, the chapter focuses on carbon dioxide targets, and explores how sectoral and local targets can be set.

Definition and brief history of environmental targets

Environmental targets describe qualitative or quantitative environmental levels to be achieved in a particular area by a certain time. In the context of the policy-implementation process, they generally represent points of reference or 'staging points', as opposed to specific end-points. Environmental targets may relate to environmental levels established by scientific investigation (*e.g.* the dose-response characteristics of pollutants and health), attitudinal surveys (*e.g.* quality of landscape), or a combination of the two (*e.g.* acceptable levels of noise). Environmental targets, then, represent a qualitative or quantitative statement of aspirations about the state of the environment and the quality of life.

The nature of existing targets varies considerably. Some are fixed, aimed at clearly specified objectives, whilst others are 'rolling'. The sanctions behind targets also vary; some have legal status and are backed by penalties; some form part of international obligations or agreements; and others are more indicative (House of Lords 1995, p.27). The attitude of government departments towards setting targets is similarly variable. The Department of the Environment has made efforts to set out a multiplicity of targets in policy areas for which it is primarily responsible, whilst targets from some other departments have been less forthcoming (House of Lords 1995, pp.27-28).

The role of targets in the policy-implementation process

Agreement of the 1992 Rio Declaration on Environment and Development and adoption of Agenda 21 commits the UK to the concept of sustainable development in all areas of policy. The UK government has set out its approach to sustainable development in all policy areas in its Strategy for Sustainable Development (UK Government 1994). Government planning guidance highlights the importance of the planning system to achieving the objectives of sustainable development, stating that 'the planning system, and the preparation of development plans in particular, can contribute to the objectives of sustainable development' (Department of the Environment 1992).

The concept of sustainable development has led to a prominent role for environmental targets in several stages of the policy-implementation process. Figure 5.1 illustrates the main stages of an environmental objectives-led policy-implementation process[1], and shows that the derivation of environmental targets and indicators is a key part of the process, following on from the definition of sustainability objectives. Not apparent from Figure 5.1 is the importance of environmental targets at different stages of the policy-implementation process. These include policy development, policy appraisal, policy implementation, policy assessment/review, environmental auditing, and are discussed in more detail below.

The role of targets in policy development is set out in PPG12 which states that development plans must begin by setting out the main aims, objectives and targets, and the strategy for achieving them, and goes on to say that 'objectives and targets of the plan need to be clearly stated and it should be made clear how the plan's policies and proposals relate to them' (Department of the Environment 1992).

Jacobs (1993, p.37) in setting out a vision of a more sustainable planning system follows a similar line, stating that environmental objectives should act as a framework for development plans and, together with indicators and targets, should precede and inform the key policies of the plan. English Nature (1994, p.37) state that targets should be used to express environmental limits in the development plan, and to set out a framework for developing policies.

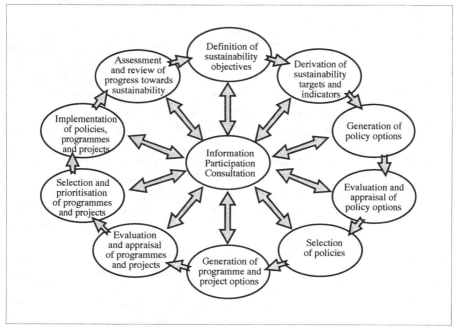

**Figure 5.1   An environmental objectives-led policy
Implementation process**

All local planning authorities now have to carry out policy appraisal (see Baker 1996 for example). PPG12 sets out this requirement, stating that local planning authorities must appraise the environmental implications of policies and proposals in their development plans, as part of the plan preparation process (Department of the Environment 1992). The role of targets in the appraisal process is described in the Department of the Environment's Environmental Appraisal of Development Plans Good Practice Guide, and identifies environmental targets as important to the appraisal process by providing benchmarks against which policies can be appraised (Department of the Environment 1993, p.12). The Royal Commission on Environmental Pollution recently recommended establishing of environmental targets to provide a framework for the environmental appraisal of transport policies (1994, p.155).

The value of targets in policy implementation is discussed in the EU Expert Group on the Urban Environment's European Sustainable Cities Report (EU Expert

Group on the Urban Environment 1994). Two important functions of targets in the implementation of policy, it contends, are securing commitment to a direction of change and helping to achieve policy goals. The report states that the effective implementation of policy depends on establishing the direction and rate of change, using indicators and targets. It appears from research into road safety targets that more ambitious targets are associated with more successful achievement of objectives, by securing more commitment and/or resources for the achievement of the objectives (Box 1).

Targets are also useful in the assessment and review stage of policy-implementation process. The EU Expert Group on the Urban Environment argue that targets are an integral part of policy assessment and review, providing 'staging points' against which policy performance can be measured (EU Expert Group on the Urban Environment 1994). Similar views are expressed by Barton and Bruder (1995, p.28) in setting out a model of environmental assessment of local government policies, arguing that policy assessment is made easier with explicit environmental targets and indicators.

Outside the policy-implementation process illustrated in Figure 5.1, but closely allied to it, is the process of local government environmental auditing - monitoring the state of the local environment and establishing the impacts of the organisation's activities. Environmental targets also have an important role in this process. Many of the targets used in the policy-implementation process described above can be used in the environmental auditing process, and vice versa. Environmental targets find application in a number of different aspects of environmental auditing, including state of the environment reporting (recommended in the Department of the Environment's Planning Policy Guidance Note 23 on Planning and Pollution Control), the review of internal practices (part of the Eco Management and Audit Scheme) and policy impact assessment (and also a stage in strategic environmental appraisal).

To summarise the role of targets in the policy-implementation process, a quote from David Begg, Chairman of Lothian Regional Council's Transportation Committee, who speaks from experience of transport targets in Lothian:

Once you have targets, your whole strategy will become geared towards achieving them, and they begin to change the philosophy of the whole organisation. They give you something to aim for, and allow feedback on progress. Whenever a proposal comes forward, the question is asked 'will this help us to meet our target' (Stringer 1995, p.13)

The target setting process

The process of developing and deriving environmental targets is at least as political as it is scientific. Jacobs (1993, pp.17-18) observes that:

limits are not always absolute or objectively 'discoverable'. The environment's capacities are not always fixed, and they cannot always be scientifically defined. Science can provide useful (if uncertain) information, particularly on factors such as 'sustainable' extraction rates for renewable resources or the 'critical loads' of pollutants at which serious damage to ecosystems is caused. But scientific evidence does not by itself make a judgement on society's goals. Ultimately environmental capacities depend on what society believes to be tolerable, for itself and future generations.

Thus, environmental targets should be developed in a systematic way, based on sound environmental data, and determined by participation and consultation on public aspirations about the state of the environment and quality of life.

BOX 1. ROAD SAFETY TARGETS IN NORWAY

National road safety targets have been adopted in various countries in recent years. These include Denmark, Finland, France, Great Britain, the Netherlands, Norway and Sweden. Targets have also been adopted at a local level in some of these countries. In Norway, road safety targets have been set by a number of county authorities. These are described by Elvik (1993) in a study of the relationship between targets and accidents.

Targets were classified into three categories according to their type and ambitiousness: highly ambitious quantitative; less ambitious quantitative; and qualitative targets. Elvik presents the case that counties which set quantified targets were more successful in reducing the road accident rate than counties which set qualitative targets. Of the counties setting quantitative targets, the ones with highly ambitious targets achieved a larger reduction in road accidents. The study shows that road safety is associated with the type of target, the ambitiousness of the target, and the level road safety spending in the county (a link between these three factors seems likely).

The chief policy implication of the study, according to Elvik, is that the adoption of ambitious targets can assist the policy-implementation process by enabling priorities to be set more effectively, and schemes implemented more successfully.

The derivation of local environmental indicators and targets follows from the definition of sustainability objectives (Figure 5.1). An example of a process for generating environmental indicators, involving the identification of the main environmental, social and economic components of sustainable development, is outlined by the Local Government Management Board (1994). In selecting environmental indicators, consideration should be given to their relevance to policy objectives. Consider the objective of reducing pollution and resource use in energy generation, for example (one of the targets outlined in Box 2). A target for increasing the *quantity* of energy generated by non-fossil fuel sources may be set. This is not the same, however, as a target for increasing the *proportion* of energy generated by non-fossil fuel sources, which is not the same as a target for reducing overall energy consumption. (Moreover, non-fossil fuel sources include nuclear fuels, and a target to increase the quantity of energy generated from non-fossil fuel sources could be seen as a sanction for nuclear energy.) Although similar, each indicator may show different responses to the same policy, and careful selection is needed. Consideration should also be given to the availability, measurability or calculability of indicator data, and the compatibility and comparability with other local and/or national indicators when selecting local environmental indicators (see UNA 1992 Measuring Sustainability).

Having selected environmental indicators (the process has been described elsewhere by Pinfield 1996), target levels can be established. In some cases (but not all) it may be possible to base local targets on existing national environmental targets or environmental standards (such as EU 'guide values' and 'limit values' of air pollutants). Setting targets requires striking the balance between unrealistically ambitious and undemandingly achievable levels. There is no point in setting targets which would be achieved in their absence, or in setting excessive, unrealistic targets which may discourage any progress towards achieving them. Target setting requires reliable baseline data and a system for monitoring progress towards the target. Local authorities may wish to adopt target levels set by external organisations (*e.g.* World Health Organisation, European Union, Department of the Environment) or adapt them to reflect local conditions. English Nature (1994, p.38) suggest, however, that local authorities targets should be at least compatible with those set by other organisations.

It should be noted that environmental targets may not always be complementary, and the interrelation between targets should be carefully examined before they are adopted. Targets for urban greenspace, for example, may conflict with targets for infill housing in urban areas. Banister (1995, p.456) suggests a hierarchy or priority list of targets may be useful for assessing and comparing the contribution of different measures towards meeting a range of targets.

Examples of environmental targets used in development plans are illustrated below (Box 2). Guidelines for the inclusion of environmental targets in development plans has been set out by English Nature (1994, p.39). They propose that targets for all environmental issues should be selected and set out at the front of the plan. Policies which assist, and which hinder, the achievement of each target should then be identified. Other action required to achieve the environmental targets but outside the scope of the development plan should also be outlined, including other internal sections or departments (such as those with responsibility for transport, environmental health, waste, minerals or conservation) and external organisations (such as UDCs, pollution agencies, neighbouring authorities and other tiers of government). It is recommended that the relevant targets are restated at the beginning of each development plan chapter.

**BOX 2. EXAMPLES OF THE TYPE OF ENVIRONMENTAL
TARGETS USED IN DEVELOPMENT PLANS**
Source: English Nature 1994

Type of Target   **Example**

Energy Consumption   To reduce CO_2 emissions by *(quantity/percent)*
                            from buildings and industry by *(date)*

Energy Generation   To increase the amount of energy generated from
                            non-fossil fuel sources by *(quantity/percent)* by
                            (date)

Waste Management   To reduce the amount of waste landfilled to
                            (quantity/percent) by *(date)*

Air Quality   To achieve, as a minimum, EU air quality guide
                            values by *(date)*

Water Quality   To increase the number of Class 1 rivers and
                            waterways by *(quantity/percent)* by *(date)*

Wildlife & Habitats   To increase the amount of woodland by
                            (quantity/percent) by *(date)*

Landscape   To conserve and enhance the character of a
                            specified landscape

Carbon dioxide targets

Carbon dioxide targets are examined in closer detail in this section for several reasons. Firstly, there is a national CO_2 target, and a number of local authorities in the UK are developing local CO_2 targets to meet their part of this target. Secondly, research suggests there are absolute limits to CO_2 emissions beyond which adverse environmental impacts occur as a result of climate change (*e.g.* Houghton *et al* 1990, 1992; UK Climate Impacts Review Group, 1991), which arguably makes target setting more necessary. A third reason is that CO_2 targets serve as a general example of other environmental targets. This section begins by identifying the details of national CO_2 target in the UK, comparing it against CO_2

targets from other countries. Local CO_2 targets are then examined, and some reasons for their development. Sectoral CO_2 targets are also considered, and compared against targets from other countries.

The Climate Change Convention commits the UK to stabilising its CO_2 emissions to, 1990 levels by 2000. On the basis of recent government forecasts (Department of Trade and Industry 1995), achievement of this target seems highly likely. The forecasts indicate, however, that UK CO_2 emissions are set to increase above 1990 levels sometime between 2000 and 2015 (according to different scenarios of economic growth and fuel prices), and there is currently no target for UK CO_2 emissions after 2000. The UK recently called for a 5-10% reduction of greenhouse gas emissions in all developed nations by 2010 at the first conference of parties to the UN Climate Change Convention in Berlin, but no target was agreed and the UK has not seen fit to adopt such a target independently. Several countries have established their own CO_2 reduction targets beyond 2000: these include Australia, Canada, Denmark, France and Germany (Owens and Cope 1992, p.14). Denmark, for example, has set stringent targets seeking to reduce national CO_2 emissions by 20% between 1988 and 2005 (Danish Ministry of Environment and Energy 1993).

Local CO_2 targets now form part of some development plans, as well as other local authority activities such as Local Agenda 21 initiatives, energy management schemes, environmental projects and transport plans. For some authorities, the incentive to set local CO_2 targets has been motivated by Friends of the Earth's 'Climate Resolution' initiative. Launched in 1994, it calls on local authorities to reduce CO_2 emissions by 30% between 1990 and 2005, and develop a strategy for achieving the target (Box 3). By mid 1995, twenty local authorities had adopted the resolution (Friends of the Earth 1995).

BOX 3. FRIENDS OF THE EARTH'S CLIMATE RESOLUTION
(Source: Friends of the Earth 1994)

Friends of the Earth are asking local authorities to adopt the resolution stating that:

'This local authority sets a target to achieve by the year 2005 a 30% reduction from 1990 levels of emissions of carbon dioxide due to energy and transport use in the authority's geographical area, and undertakes to develop a detailed strategy to achieve this target within 12 months of adopting this resolution.'

In addition to national and local CO_2 targets, there is an increasing amount of interest and activity in developing sectoral CO_2 targets. Like other sectoral environmental targets, they provide a focused way of developing policies to achieve environmental objectives. In Denmark, for example, specific CO_2 targets for different sectors have been developed. The target for CO_2 emissions from transport, for example, is the stabilisation of emissions to 1988 levels by 2005, and 25% reduction by 2030 (Danish Ministry of Transport 1993). A comprehensive set of sectoral environmental targets has not so far been developed in the UK.

The role of environmental indicators for the transport sector have been discussed by the Secretary of State for Transport in the Department of Transport's series of national transport debates (Department of Transport 1995), where a number of problems and difficulties in setting sectoral targets were identified. Transport targets but were not ruled out, however, and more dialogue on the subject was invited (*ibid*). The Danish sectoral targets for CO_2 emissions from transport contrast strongly with UK CO_2 forecasts which indicate an increase in CO_2 emissions from transport by 10-23% between 1990 and 2005 (Department of Trade and Industry 1995).

Some local authorities in Denmark, including the City of Copenhagen have developed sectoral CO_2 targets, where the combination of targets amounts to an overall CO_2 reduction target of 30% between 1988 and 2005, exceeding the Danish national CO_2 target (Danish Ministry of Environment and Energy 1995, pp.22-23). In the UK, few local authorities, have set specific CO_2 targets for each sector. Cambridgeshire County Council is an exception. The County Council has set a 30% CO_2 reduction target for the domestic, transport and energy generation sectors (Cambridgeshire County Council 1995).

Little has been written on the process of developing local or sectoral environmental targets in the UK. Literature is more widely available in the health sector for the derivation of local health targets from the national level. Some of the basic principles can be transferred from the health sector and applied to environmental targets. The following list, for example, has been adapted from a Department of Health publication (Department of Health 1993), and outlines some of the important considerations in determining local targets. In establishing local or sectoral CO_2 emission targets, the following factors should be considered:

- local baseline data of CO_2 emissions by sector;
- local trends in CO_2 emissions by sector;
- likely changes in local trends;
- characteristics of the sectors;
- the effect of local policy changes;
- the effectiveness of local policy changes (in terms of costs and benefits); and
- the local effect of likely national policy changes.

Having established this information, there is no single method of selecting local or sectoral targets. There are a variety of approaches for establishing targets, with different advantages, disadvantages and outcomes. National CO_2 trends and forecasts are used as the basis for establishing sectoral CO_2 targets (Table 5.1). Three sets of targets are presented in Table 5.2, all with the same aim of reducing overall CO_2 emissions by 30% between 1990 and 2005.

73

Table 5.1
UK carbon dioxide (CO_2) sectoral emissions trends and forecasts

SECTOR	CO_2 EMISSIONS [2]			CO_2 FORECAST [2]	
	1990 CO_2 levels (MTonnes)	1995 CO_2 levels (MTonnes)	% change 1990-1995	2005 CO_2 forecast [3] MTonnes)	% change 1990-2005
Industry	48.0	42.9	-11	48.9	+2
Domestic	41.7	40.2	-4	38.4	-8
Road Transport	33.2	35.2	+6	40.5	+22
Other Transport	5.0	4.9	-2	5.3	+6
Commercial etc	23.0	21.3	-7	22.9	0
Other	7.4	6.3	-15	6.0	-19
Total	**158.3**	**150.8**	**-5**	**162.0**	**+2**

Table 5.2
Different approaches for setting sectoral CO_2 targets

SECTOR	CO_2 TARGETS #1		CO_2 TARGETS #2		CO_2 TARGETS #3	
	2005 CO_2 target (MTonnes)	%change 1990 -2005	2005 CO_2 target (MTonnes)	%change 1990 -2005	2005 CO_2 target (MTonnes)	%change 1990 -2005
Industry	33.6	-30	30.8	-36	33.4	-30
Domestic	29.2	-30	29.6	-29	26.3	-37
Road Transport	23.2	-30	26.8	-19	27.7	-17
Other Transport	3.5	-30	3.6	-27	3.6	-27
Commercial etc	16.1	-30	15.5	-33	15.7	-32
Other	5.2	-30	4.4	-40	4.1	-45
Total	**110.8**	**-30**	**110.8**	**-30**	**110.8**	**-30**

The first approach to setting sectoral targets simply involves the equal reduction of emissions (by 30%) from all sectors. The second set of reduction targets is related to previous trends in CO_2 emissions (between 1990 and 1995 in this case). The sectoral targets are determined by the difference between the overall reduction in CO_2 levels required between 1995 and 2005 (25% since a 5% reduction was achieved between 1990 and 1995), and the change in sectoral CO_2 levels between

1990 and 1995. The third set of targets is related to the target date forecasts. The targets are based on equal reductions in forecast levels for 2005 to achieve an overall 30% reduction.

The first set of targets, based on an equal percentage reduction in CO_2 for all sectors, does not take into account factors such as previous trends or future forecasts, or the varying level of difficulty of different sectors to achieve equal reductions. The second set of targets, based on past trends in CO_2 emissions, seeks to achieve larger CO_2 reductions in sectors where emissions have been decreasing (*e.g.* the industrial sector) and smaller reductions in sectors whebe emissions have been increasing (*e.g.* the transport sector). Like the first approach, this does not take into account the varying level of difficulty of different sectors to achieve these reductions. Sectors that have achieved larger reductions in the past are not necessarily the ones which can sustain the largest reductions in the future. The third approach, involving forecasting future sectoral emission levels and applying equal percentage reductions to all sectors again does not account for the varying level of difficulty that different sectors may experience in achieving proportionally similar reductions.

The above examples illustrate a few of many approaches to sectoral setting. Similar techniques can also be used to determine local targets from national ones. It is evident that each technique provides a different set of targets, and should be used as an aid to target setting, rather than a definitive prescription. To re-emphasise a point made earlier, the process of developing and deriving environmental targets is at least as political as it is scientific. Targets are not always absolute or objectively 'discoverable'. Scientific analysis should be used to inform rather than prescribe the target setting process.

Conclusions

Environmental targets are relatively recent policy tools which are becoming increasingly important not just in planning policy, but all areas of policy. Targets are not ends in themselves, but useful tools in the policy-implementation process. They are a means of achieving more sustainable policies in all policy areas, and have particular value in focusing attention on the link between the policy-implementation process and outcomes. The role of environmental targets in land-use planning includes policy development, policy appraisal, policy implementation, policy assessment/review, and environmental auditing. Environmental targets may not always be complementary, and the interrelation between targets should be carefully examined before they are adopted. A hierarchy or priority list of targets may be useful for assessing and comparing the contribution of different measures towards meeting a range of targets. The process of target setting is at least as political as it is scientific. Environmental targets should be developed in a systematic way, based on sound environmental data, and determined by participation and consultation on public aspirations about the state of the environment and quality of life. Targets are already being included in development plans, although there is still considerable amount of work to be done in identifying the more suitable types of environmental targets, target levels, and scales of application (local, regional, national, *etc.*). A considerable amount of work is now going on in local authorities and elsewhere to establish this information.

Notes

1 The environmental objectives-led policy process is frequently advocated as a way of producing more environmentally sustainable policies (*e.g.* Jacobs 1993; English Nature 1994; Royal Commission on Environmental Pollution 1994; McLaren and Bosworth 1994).

2 Source: Department of Trade and Industry (1995).

3 Energy forecasts based on a scenario of central growth in GDP and low fuel prices (Source: Department of Trade and Industry 1995).

References

Baker, J. (1996), 'Environmental Appraisal of Development Plans', in Farthing, S (ed.), *Evaluating Local Environmental Policy*, Avebury: Aldershot.

Banister, D. (1995), 'Transport and the Environment', *Town Planning Review*, Vol. 66, No. 4, pp.453-458.

Barton, H. and Bruder, N. (eds.), (1995), *A Guide to Local Environmental Auditing*, Earthscan: London.

Cambridgeshire County Council (1995), *Draft Carbon Dioxide Reduction Strategy*, Corporate Planning, Cambridgeshire County Council: Cambridge.

Climate Impacts Review Group (1991), *The Potential Effects of Climate Change in the United Kingdom*, HMSO: London.

Danish Ministry of Environment and Energy (1993), *Energy 2000 - follow up*, Ministry of Environment and Energy: Copenhagen.

Danish Ministry of Environment and Energy (1995), *The Urban Environment and Planning - Examples from Denmark*, Ministry of Environment and Energy: Copenhagen.

Danish Ministry of Transport (1993), *Transport 2005*, Ministry of Transport: Copenhagen.

Department of Health (1993), *Local Target Setting. A Discussion Paper*, NHS Management Executive: Leeds.

Department of the Environment (1992), *Planning Policy Guidance 12. Development Plans and Regional Planning Guidance*, HMSO: London.

Department of the Environment (1993), *Environmental Appraisal of Development Plans. A Good Practice Guide*, HMSO: London.

Department of the Environment (1994), *Planning Policy Guidance 23. Planning and Pollution Control*, HMSO: London.

Department of Trade and Industry (1995), *Energy Projections for the UK. Energy Paper 65*, HMSO: London.

Department of Transport (1995), *Transport: The Way Ahead*, Department of Transport: London.

Elvik, R. (1993), 'Quantified Road Safety Targets' *Accident Analysis and Prevention*, Vol. 25, No. 5, pp.569-583.

English Nature (1994), *Sustainability in Practice*, English Nature: Peterborough.

EU Urban Environment Expert Group on the Urban Environment (1994), *European Sustainable Cities*, EU: Brussels.

Friends of the Earth (1994), *The Climate Resolution: A Guide to Local Authority Action*, Friends of the Earth: London.

Friends of the Earth (1995), *The Climate Resolution Update. Number 2*, Friends of the Earth: London.

Houghton, J., Jenkins, G. and Ephraims, J. (eds.), (1990), *Climate Change. The IPCC Assessment*, Cambridge University Press: Cambridge.

House of Lords (1995), *Report from the Select Committee on Sustainable Development*, Vol. 1, HMSO: London.

Jacobs, M. (1993), *Sense and Sustainability*, Council for the Protection of Rural England: London.

Local Government Management Board (1994), *Sustainability Indicators Research Project. Report of Phase One*, LGMB: Luton.

McLaren, D. and Bosworth, T. (1994), *Planning for the Planet*, Friends of the Earth: London.

Owens, S. and Cope, D. (1992), *Land Use Planning Policy and Climate Change*, HMSO: London.

Pinfield, G. (1996), 'Sustainability indicators: a new tool for evaluation', in Farthing, S. (ed.), *Evaluating Local Environmental Policy*, Avebury: Aldershot.

Royal Commission on Environmental Pollution (1994), *Transport and the Environment*, HMSO: London.

Stringer, B. (1995), 'Setting Targets for Transport: Policymaking by Numbers?', *Local Transport Today*, Vol. 166, pp.12-13.

UK Government (1994), *Sustainable Development. The UK Strategy*, HMSO: London.

UK Government (1995), *Government Response to the Lords Select Committee Report on Sustainable Development*, HMSO: London.

United Nations Association (1992), *Measuring Sustainability*, UNA: New York.

6 Environmental capacity and sustainable urban form

Hugh Barton

Introduction

Arguments over environmental capacity are being used increasingly to justify constraints on settlement pattern and urban form. But there is as yet no generally accepted and robust technique for the definition of capacity. This paper will draw on work undertaken in preparation for the DoE guide to the 'Environmental Appraisal of Development Plans' (DoE 1993) and for the UWE/LGMB guide to 'Sustainable Settlements' (Barton et al 1995) to argue that the concept of environmental capacity as currently employed is dangerous because it tends to be partial and is open to hijacking by specific interests. Recent examples of appraisal and capacity estimates will be cited to support this view. The paper will then develop ideas for a more robust approach, building on the outlines in 'Sustainable Settlements' (Barton et al 1995). In essence this approach stresses the need for a comprehensive view of capacity in relation to all elements of environmental stock, and a recognition that planning for 'sustainable development' - not purely environmental sustainability - demands explicit treatment of social, economic, global and local environmental priorities.

The conclusion of the paper will relate this approach back to the issue of settlement form and specifically to the examples of recent work on environmental capacity, suggesting that in each case the outcome could be different. Further that proper consideration of social, economic and environmental thresholds would put a question mark against the simple assumptions of the compact city debate.

The urban form debate

Arguments over the future shape and disposition of settlements have become polarized. On the one hand there are the advocates of the 'compact city', and on the other the devotees of new settlements. Growth and change in the compact city occur by renewal and intensification rather than spread and scatter. It therefore relies on a complimentary strategy of rural restraint. Growth of outlying commuter settlements is deterred in order to avoid an increase in longer distance trips and focus the attention of developers on the central town (Barton et al 1995, p.94). The object of the compact city strategy is not only to reduce transport energy use and emissions it is also - in the view of the Green Paper on the Urban Environment (Commission of European Communities 1990) - a means of achieving cultural, social and economic regeneration of declining urban areas, overcoming blight and pollution, recreating and sustaining a vibrant city life. The underlying belief is that 'cities are good for us' (Sherlock 1991). The Department of Environment to a significant extent, appears to agree (PPG13 1994); and empirical work supports the view that higher density cities are more energy-efficient (Hillman and Whalley 1983; Newman and Kenworthy 1989). By contrast the decentralisers, with the Town and Country Planning Association in the van, argue that the vision of the compact city is not realistic, and decentralisation from cities to small towns and villages is a trend too powerful to counter (Breheny 1992). On this model falling urban densities offer the chance to green the cities while new and expanded rural settlements are planned for aesthetic delight and local autonomy. The image conveyed (though rarely seen) is of small scale communities, in harmony with their environment, reliant on renewable energy, dealing with their own wastes, and linked to the global village by telecommunications (Ecologist 1972).

Both these pictures have their attractions and are reflected in the options that are being considered by local authorities in the local and structure plans. In Gloucester, for example, the debate is between the further expansion of Gloucester (maybe at the expense of the green belt between Cheltenham and Gloucester) and the designation of a significant new town sufficiently separate to possess some autonomy. In Humberside the review of the Structure Plan (suspended pending reorganisation) pointed to the discrepancy between the *stated* strategy of concentration and the *actual* strategy of dispersal resulting from incremental decision-making. In Wiltshire the County wish to reduce the need to travel by concentrating growth around Swindon, while the Districts desire 'balanced' growth to maintain the vitality of all the smaller towns.

Yet there is more than a suspicion that these polarized models of settlement patterns are not telling the whole story. It is difficult to maintain the practicality of the compact city ideal in the face of household formation trends, housing need forecasts and expressed consumer preferences. Conversely it is difficult to justify the sustainability of decentralisation in the light of evidence about small settlements, high levels of car ownership and resulting emissions (Bannister 1992). It may well be that both represent unrealistic visions, and for solutions we should look instead at the places where most people live - ie. the suburbs. John Winter and Stuart Farthing take up a similar position on the necessity for continued suburban expansion in a later chapter in this volume. They suggest that UK government policy advice which advocates either very large new settlements or urban infill should be reviewed.

Capacity and form

Into this ongoing debate on settlement patterns comes the concept of environmental capacity. Whereas urban form is concerned with the *dynamic* of human settlements, environmental capacity is concerned with the *constraints* on settlement growth, and, in the guise of 'carrying capacity', with the ability of natural ecosystem to support human activity. The two concepts are therefore complementary. The guide to Sustainable Settlements argues that both are also necessary in the planning of sustainable development (Barton et al 1995, ch. 4). The questions arise as to whether environmental capacity *is* being defined and used in such a way that it is helpful to urban form decisions; and secondly, what implications there might be for the great urban form debate. We return to these two questions after a detailed review of the state of the art.

Divergent interpretations of capacity

The concept of environmental capacity is seductive. It holds out the tempting prospect of being able to identify objective limits to growth, of being able to declare 'thus far and no more'. It is being used by environmental interests and planning authorities to ward off development pressures and safeguard environmental quality. Like 'sustainable development', it has become in the 1990's a catch phrase, almost a talisman, recited by planners and environmentalists as token of green probity.

Yet, unlike 'sustainable development', there is no generally accepted definition of environmental capacity. Nor is there any technique currently available that can deliver a robust and comprehensive assessment of capacity. On the contrary the term is being used by different people in different contexts to mean completely different things.

The range of perspectives on environmental capacity, and the linked (but not synonymous) concept of carrying capacity, in part reflects simply the remits of different organisations. The National Rivers Authority is concerned with the capacity of the hydrological system to absorb human activity and provide healthy water supply without long-term damage. The Council for the Protection of Rural England is concerned with preserving open country for its own sake. Nature conservation interests identify the threshold of unacceptable impact on fragile or valued ecosystems. For such agencies the partial view is perhaps a necessary concomitant of their particular roles. The distortion comes only if they then make *general* claims about reaching or exceeding environmental carrying capacity. Such claims are a kind of slight of hand, raising perhaps exaggerated fears and undermining the credibility of the concept.

Potentially more serious is the way in which planning authorities are using the term. While environmental agencies are recognised as having a particular stance, local authorities are supposed to adopt a 'balanced' and dispassionate overview, planning in the best interests of all constituencies. Yet current practice as reviewed by Grigson for the House Builders Federation, reflects often a one-sided approach, and a cavalier attitude to scientific justification (Grigson 1995). The divergence in interpretation is marked. There are two contrasting - and inherently opposed - positions taken by local authorities, one concerned essentially with the capacity of the *towns*, the other with the capacity of the *countryside*. There is rarely proper acknowledgement of the divergence or of the implications of adopting one and not the other on questions of settlement pattern and form.

Assessments of urban capacity

The first point to make about urban (or built) environmental capacity is that while the term seems new the idea is not. Planning authorities have routinely considered the capacity of building stock and infrastructure and set limits on the rate of urban change in the interests of conservation. The central issue is the physical capacity of the urban built environment to provide properly for people's physical, social and psychological needs.

Currently the most influential capacity estimate concerns housing. Structure Plan authorities conventionally estimate the capacity of the existing housing stock, making assumptions about household size, families sharing, dwelling subdivision, urban renewal and so on, and then subsequently rely on this figure to calculate the need for greenfield development. There are two important things to note about this process: first, that it works from a starting point (however inadequately defined) of *human need*; second, that the estimates depend not only on the physical attributes of the housing stock but also assumptions about life-styles, market pressures and planning policy. The centrality of policy cannot be over-emphasised: the estimate of capacity *incorporates* policies on housing densities, infill, subdivisions and the renewal of brownfield sites (though sometimes in a rather mechanistic way). If urban intensification, rather than urban spread, is to be the rule - in line with the 'compact city' - then the housing need calculations have to reflect this.

Some city authorities, at least, are actively trying to increase the use of brownfield sites and achieve high densities on urban renewal schemes. But housing need estimates are still outstripping the resulting housing supply estimates and leading to 'green field' release on a major scale (eg. Bristol), putting a question mark over the practicality of the 'compact city' ideal.

Another important angle on urban environmental capacity is *perceptual*. While the capacity of roads may be defined by maximum possible traffic flows (themselves affected by traffic management policies), it may also be related to 'acceptable' levels of environmental impact. Buchanan, in his seminal report on Traffic in Towns (1963), used it in this sense. He emphasised the significance of being able to talk on the street without shouting, and being able to cross the street without undue delay or intimidation by traffic.

81

This early work provides the background to the most ambitious study of urban capacity so far, incorporating both physical and perceptual aspects. The recent study of Chester, undertaken by Ove Arup on behalf of Cheshire County Council, the City Council and English Heritage, has attempted to take on board most of the relevant variables (Ove Arup 1993; Cheshire County Council et al. 1994). It tries to match physical capacity (of streets, pedestrian areas etc) with perceptual capacity - whether people *feel* overcrowded, intimidated by traffic or offended by fumes and noise. At the same time it embraces aesthetic values, examining the potential impact of growth not only on listed buildings, conservation areas and green space, but also the broader aesthetic of the city - its distinctive shape and form. Strangely the capacity of the housing stock did not form part of the study. The study is notable for attempting to deal not only with environmental issues but social and economic (eg. the buoyancy of the shopping centre) as well.

The conclusion is that there is 'considerable scope for change and controlled growth in Chester without damaging those things that make Chester special'. But the report stresses that any change must be highly selective and geared to quality. It suggests that some development should be deflected to other locations in the sub-region. It suggests further edge-of-town shopping proposals on condition that they are not so big as to threaten the primacy of Chester's retail centre. It does not examine the impact of such decentralisation on the sub-region or on critical aspects of global environmental stock. More on these issues later.

Rural environmental capacity

While the Chester study is being held up by the planning fraternity as the state of the art on environmental capacity, a completely different approach is being widely employed in relation to open space, wildlife and countryside issues. At its simplest, and with a long pedigree, this approach can be equated with *sieve-mapping*. 'Critical' and 'constant' environmental capital (habitats, landscapes, water and mineral resources, etc) are mapped and then act as absolute or negotiable constraints on the siting of new development.

The adoption of principles of sustainable development has given a new fillip to sieve-mapping. More varied and detailed information is being gathered (in State of the Environment reports) and recorded in sophisticated computer-mapping systems. Environmental agencies such as English Nature are pressurising for the grading of designated areas as 'critical' stock, and therefore inviolate.

If some zones are inviolate it means, of course, that other areas. perhaps only marginally less significant, are more liable to be 'violated'. The Countryside Commission interprets sustainability as relating to 'the overall quality of the countryside' and its enhancement (Countryside Commission 1993). So there are important issues over 'whose countryside' and what most needs conservation (Environmental Resources Management 1995).

The other new ingredient in estimates of rural capacity is the concept of 'carrying capacity'. Some authorities have latched on to this in order to justify a Canute-type stance in relation to new greenfield development. Hampshire County Council in their draft Structure Plan adopted the principle that all open land is critical environmental capital and sacrosanct. This absolutist attitude was politically driven and had strong CPRE support, but it lacked any technical appraisal and ignored the impact on human need and the wider environment beyond the confines of Hampshire. It was rightly castigated by the DOEs panel following the Plan's Examination in Public (Grigson 1995).

Berkshire took a broader and less rigid view. It attempted to relate the carrying capacity of the County not only to landscape and countryside impacts but also to water supply, energy use, timber and mineral resources, and levels of air and river pollution. Public opinion played a major and explicit role. Berkshire argued that its environmental constraints were so severe that it was justified in downgrading the goal of satisfying housing needs, and in so doing it went against both national planning guidance and the obligation in the Brundtland definition of sustainable development to meet todays needs (Grigson 1995).

The potential implications of such estimates of rural capacity for settlement patterns are clear. Environmental capacity is being used to resist the further development of existing towns or the creation of new 'rural' settlements. In effect the concept is being hijacked for NIMBY purposes, often with little regard to wider environmental or social impacts. 'Capacity' is taken to imply a kind of absolutist approach to human ecology, giving a spurious sense of scientific objectivity to what may be a valid subjective view of existing inhabitants. This absolutism can thus be very politically attractive, allowing an area to be officially designated as 'full'.

Capacity of what, for whom?

The problem with both the urban and the rural variants of environmental capacity is that they are partial: partial in the sense that they promote certain interests without considering others, and partial in relation to the agenda of sustainability. Hampshire was partial in raising one environmental criteria to the status of green idol and ignoring both global sustainability and the local impact on people.

The Cheshire study also (and despite its generally high quality) begs many questions. It ignores the possible impact of urban environmental protection on the environment of the nearby smaller towns and countryside. In supporting over time some degree of dispersal, and also car-based edge-of-town retailing, it is helping justify increased car dependence and longer trip lengths. Thus it is partial in its concentration on Chester alone and its focus on local environmental quality at the possible expense of global resources.

Chester, Hampshire and Berkshire are not autonomous. They cannot be treated as islands, sufficient unto themselves. If development within their confines is unduly restricted then problems are simply exported to neighbouring authorities, and people may be forced to live in inconvenient locations, increasing their own costs and transport-related global emissions.

So the central question, when faced with the term 'environmental capacity', is capacity of what, for whom? None of the examples examined can make any valid claim to a holistic view of the environment, or a sustainable view of human communities. Such limited versions of 'capacity' should not be used by themselves to determine settlement patterns, concentration or dispersal. Much more honest, therefore, to avoid *implying* such an overview. Rather, adopt more precise and limited terms. If the issue is the capacity of heathland to absorb human recreation without damage to the diversity of its species and ecosystems, then perhaps that is better called 'heathland capacity'. If it is the capacity of a water catchment area to sustain human activity, then perhaps that is better called 'water catchment capacity'. If it is the capacity of a historic town the accept growth without destroying its character, then call it 'heritage capacity'. In that way we can avoid misleading (and even deceitful) implications of having reached an objective, comprehensive and definitive measure of capacity.

Measuring capacity

It is arguable that even such specific capacities as those above are not objective measures - they may be rather statements of policy. In the case of the heathland there are objective measures of habitat health and species diversity; and the relationship of those indicators to causal factors (such as loss to farmland, visitor pressure, pollution levels or climatic variation) are a matter for informed judgement and research. But the decision on those grounds to impose a capacity limit on visitors is a political one, balancing one basic value, that of freedom of access, against another, that of protecting wildlife. And once political priorities have been agreed, then the acceptable level of visitors can be profoundly affected by recreational management, eg. shifting a car park away from a fragile area, or improving certain paths, or changing the signs. At a more fundamental level, the natural ecosystems are themselves in dynamic flux, reacting to pressures, seeking new 'niche' opportunities, rarely static. The 'capacity' of the heathland, therefore, is a function of political decision, professional creativity, scientific judgment, *and* dispassionate observation of natural processes.

The 'Limits of Acceptable Change' approach, pioneered by the US Forestry Service, recognises this. It moves the discussion away from fixed limits towards quality management and the involvement of a wide range of interests in decision-making (Sidaway 1994).

The population carrying capacity of water resources in a region could on first sight appear more open to precise calculation - capable of putting a limit on growth. In certain areas of England the river and groundwater abstraction rates are unsustainable. Population and economic activity level are already, it can be argued, *over*capacity. But any defined capacity level is related to assumptions about public

84

policy and consumer behaviour. If these were altered then the carrying capacity might change as well. For example, if all new developments (in and out of town) were obliged to catch their own water for all non-drinking purposes, and treat their own sewage and ensure on-site infiltration of waste water, then the carrying capacity in relation to water would be, over time, transformed. (Incidentally I have seen prototype schemes in Denmark which achieve all of that and more.)

Some aspects of capacity *are* relatively difficult to manage. The major factor leading to the declining capacity of the existing housing stock, for example, is declining household size, itself the result of profound long-term social changes. No policy initiatives are likely to have the power to reverse that trend for the foreseeable future.

Thresholds and capacities

Given that environmental capacities are often more statements of where we are now in relation to policy and human activity, rather then objective facts, it might be better to drop the term altogether and refer instead to *thresholds*. A threshold in this context is a point or level at which action is necessary. Thresholds can sometimes be overcome by better management or new investment. The term does not imply a comprehensive view. It can be used quite precisely.

My suggestion is that the term 'threshold' should be applied when we are concerned with a particular element of environmental stock, or to a limited range of elements. So it would be appropriate in relation to the heathland example, triggering a response when the threshold is crossed. It would be appropriate in relation to the impact of growth on the character of Chester. It is altogether a more adaptable concept, and trade-offs between impacts on different facets of the environment can be made explicit. On this basis the phrase 'environmental capacity', with its grandiose implications, would be appropriate only where a systematic overview was taken.

Conclusions on the current approach to capacity

The notion of environmental capacity is being used at present in widely different ways, related to the physical capacity of land and buildings, or the sustainability of local ecosystems, or the perceived impact on local communities. The extension of capacity arguments to questions of 'carrying capacity' of the resource base is seductive. It gives the appearance of offering a kind of objective, scientific rationale to no growth or slow growth strategies. But my contention is that the idea of capacity (being 'full up') is flawed, and has real dangers. It is not only that environmental capacity arguments can become a cloak for NIMBYism (and thus lose credibility). It is that the concept of capacity gives the impression of telling the whole story, while in fact it does not. To adapt and extend the conclusion of

85

an earlier paper (Barton 1994).

- Capacity has some validity when applied to factors such as the existing building stock, where the stock is relatively stable and exogenous variables predictable.
- The concept has less validity when applied to features such as natural habitats that have innate regeneration abilities, and where policy decisions can easily alter the context (for example by changed management regimes) and thus capacity.
- The population carrying capacity of a particular town or region can only be usefully defined if that region is an island, sufficient unto itself. The island approach does not relate to normal social and economic realities.
- Rather than capacities, which suggest absolute limits, it might be more constructive to work to *thresholds* - levels of activity or population that demand careful planning and perhaps major investment before they can be breached.
- The definition of thresholds (or capacities) can usefully be informed by technical analysis, but involve judgements which are essentially political - trade-offs of one need against another need. Thresholds and capacities should therefore be recognised as *policies* or *objectives*, rather than *facts*.
- In almost all cases observed to date the assessment of 'environmental capacity' is partial, often ignoring major facets of environmental stock: particularly rural capacity estimates ignoring urban realities, and urban ignoring rural.
- Environmental capacity arguments, as used in practice at present, are likely to *distort* basic decisions on settlement/urban form strategy, and could *undermine* moves towards sustainable development.

A comprehensive approach

The requirements of a valid approach to environmental capacity are quite intimidating. Grigson recommends that the process should involve a specific study based on a comprehensive inventory of the environment and an area of study wide enough to embrace the environmental capacity of possible alternative development locations. The study should be systematic, structured, clear, and full documentation should be publically available (Grigson 1995).

One recent study attempts to take these strictures on board. The approach presented in 'Sustainable Settlements' (Barton et al 1995) centres on an 'appraisal framework' which relates elements of environmental stock to the nature and level of development impact (See Figure 6.1). The framework is comprehensive in relation to the environment, including physical, ecological and perceptual aspects, natural and human-made, urban and rural. It is organised so as to tone in with the 'global to local' approach given in the Good Practice Guide to the Environmental Appraisal of Development Plans (DoE 1993). Global climatic impact is set beside

86

Elements of Environmental Stock	GLOBAL ECOLOGY — GLOBAL ATMOSPHERE/CLIMATE					NATURAL RESOURCES			LOCAL ENVIRONMENT		
	Energy in Transport		Energy use in buildings and carbon-fixing	Biodiversity	Air quality	Water resources	Land and soil	Minerals and energy resources	Built environment	Open space	Aesthetic and cultural heritage
Constraints and Potential	Access to facilities	Transport networks									
Critical constraints	no facilities accessible or planned	no accessible and frequent public transport services available or planned	very exposed sites	SSSI's, SPA's, SAC, Ramsar sites, NNR's ancient woodlands	areas prone to unacceptable levels of air pollution	areas liable to flood	unstable land; areas prone to coastal erosion	scarce/high value reserve	fully 'built up' areas, well used and maintained	attractive, well used and accessible public open space (POS)	listed buildings; rare archeological sites; vulnerable landscapes of great value
Transferable constraints			shelter belts, woodlands, coppices	ESA's, other semi-natural habitats, wildlife corridors		areas with excessive abstraction rates; a high ground water vulnerability	allotments, established organic farmland	other reserves (substitution by conservation)		common land; locally value or potentially accessible open space	areas of great landscape value
Negotiable constraints	limited facilities accessible, but provision could be improved	currently substandard public transport services capable of improvement	North-facing slopes, trees and hedgerows	locally valued but common habitats, trees and hedgerows	mitigatable levels of pollution	water supply and drainage at capacity and area of medium ground water vulnerability	high quality soils contaminated land	potential ambient energy capture	roads/services at capacity	private open space lacking public access	National Parks; AONBs; conservation areas
Development opportunity	many facilities accessible	satisfactory level of service in terms of accessibility and frequency	gentle South-facing slopes; well-sheltered sites, potential tree planting bonus	No threat to assets		spare capacity in supply and drainage	degraded or derelict land (unless of special wildlife value)		spare capacity in roads/services: infill/renewal potential	ample and assessible open space	ugly/ monotonous urban environment
Development priority	most facilities highly accessible	good access to high quality local and sub-regional public transport services	spare capacity on CHP/DH system						empty urban buildings and brownfield sites		

Figure 6.1 The Capacity assessment framework (CAF) - an illustrative not definitive analysis

natural resources and local environmental quality. The key elements in estimating *global* impact are accessibility, movement networks and energy-efficiency, reflecting concern for improving the quality of life as well as reducing greenhouse emissions.

The implications of this comprehensive approach for the nature of capacity assessment are profound. While 'environmental capacity' is conventionally about constraints on development, the concern for quality of access and transport points to development *opportunities*. Given a proven *need* for new building, then it may sometimes be better to locate where pollution generated is minimised, rather than where impact on locally-identified environmental capital is minimised. Where necessary, a balance has to be struck, and the framework helps articulate the debate. In this, it harks back to the development potential techniques used in the 1970s.

Positive and negative impacts are further graded in the framework. In particular *critical* constraints are distinguished from *transferable* and *negotiable* constraints. Critical constraints relate to critical environmental capital or risk which should preclude any further development. Examples are SSS1s, areas liable to flooding, and locations with no facilities within walking distance (and little chance of getting any). Transferable constraints relate to protection of 'constant environmental assets', with a general presumption against development except where there is proven overriding need and the ability to replace the lost assets or substitute something at least as valuable. Examples are woodlands, open space, and (perhaps) energy resources. Negotiable constraints relate to zones affected by environmental problems, or pushing against thresholds where development can occur *only* if the problems are mitigated, thresholds overcome by investment. Examples might be contaminated land, areas of medium ground water vulnerability, substandard provision for public transport.

To succeed in practice, such distinctions would need to be written into the Development Plan, recorded accurately on maps, backed at appeal, and, where development is allowed, implemented through planning agreements.

The 'Appraisal Framework' is seen as the central organising device in a process of 'capacity' decision-making that is really just part of the development plan review process, including public and political involvement and systematic evaluation of options. It could also be seen as a means of co-ordinating and giving shape to ongoing State of the Environment surveys, with involvement of relevant environmental bodies, perhaps in the context of the Local Agenda 21 programmes.

The endemic problems of comprehensive technical procedures are the time/cost of information gathering and the risk of confusing the issues rather than clarifying them. The 'Sustainable Settlements' approach tries to minimise the time and cost by linking environmental capacity closely into other required decision processes (development plan, LA21) and providing a logic to GIS data collection which makes the results useful (and saleable!) to private sector and community agencies as well as local authorities and other official bodies. The system tries to avoid obfuscation by distinguishing very clearly between matters of *fact* (eg. the location of a SSSI, or a woodland habitat) and matters of *value* (eg. the weight put on preserving the woodland as opposed to improving access). The point of the exercise is to ensure that important aspects are not tacitly ignored, and that trade-offs between one aspect and another are explicit.

The appraisal framework can, conversely, be criticized for not being comprehensive enough. It deals with all matters environmental but not to the same extent matters social and economic, therefore failing to match the definition of 'sustainable development' which highlights providing for the social 'needs' of today and tomorrow.

The criticism is not entirely valid, however, because the framework does two things compensate for the absence of explicit social and economic criteria. Firstly it deals fully with people's immediate perceived environment, and local community/political concerns for the quality of life and of surroundings can be reflected there. Secondly, by indicating the positive as well as negative factors it does effectively address some social needs (eg. in terms of good accessibility) and economic efficiency (in terms of utilizing spare capacity).

Nevertheless gaps remain in relation to commercial viability and community impact. Critically, those factors are very powerful in the politics of local decision making, and their absence from the framework reduces credibility, and may induce users to *distort* the environment capacity criteria to encompass community or viability criteria (as we saw in Hampshire). So the proposal here is to convert the framework - at risk of added complexity - from being about environmental capacity to being more broadly about *sustainable development*. The scope of the Sustainable Development Appraisal would therefore be:

Global Impact	Natural Resources	Local Environment	Community Impact	Commercial Viability

Such an extension of scope to recognise legitimate and important facets of sustainable development has also been advocated following recent experience of Environmental Appraisal of Development Plans[1]. It has become clear that environmental appraisal (and by implication, estimates of capacity) should not be treated as a bolt-on adjunct of plan-making but should be fully integrated - as indeed required by PPG12. The concept of sustainable development provides a rationale for doing this.

There may well be problems in such an extension. The question arises, is it *possible* to identify some dispassionate indicators of community impact and commercial viability, preferably amenable to mapping?

Further research and development is needed in this sphere: the objective is to define criteria of 'social sustainability' that are not simply an expression of NIMBY politics but have some independent validity, and can thus embrace legitimate local concern in the official planning process without being in thrall to it. There may be merit in examining, for example, issues of community balance and diversity (See Barton et al 1995, p.111), of social stability, of the level of local social interaction.

Any criteria needs both to have political resonance (to validate it and draw in support) and direct relevance to the amount and nature of urban change/development.

Market criteria are probably easier to identify, and can be easily related to location. The process of identifying 'marketable' and 'developable' housing land already draws on the expertise of house builders and their agents, and this approach could be applied to commercial land as well. Establishing a relationship between the 'housing land available' calculation and environmental capacity could be very positive : it would expose the (possibly conservative) views of the house-building fraternity to wider scrutiny, and expose the developers to the sustainable implications of different locations.

Another possible economic criterion links back to the principle of accessibility. Recent research tends to confirm the intuitive assumptions that local jobs means shorter average trip lengths for the journey to work, and a higher proportion by foot and bike (Stead 1994). 'Sustainable Settlements' (Barton et al 1995) suggests use of a job ratio to measure the degree of land use mix in an area. The key threshold tentatively suggested (and requiring further validation) is 0.7 - ie. at least 7 local jobs available for every 10 local people available for work. Below that threshold the number of short walk-based work trips falls off significantly. The figure could be used as part of the environment capacity analysis to identify those areas with spare capacity for residents, or needing further commercial development to establish a reasonable balance.

The quality of our environment, and its capacity to support growth of human settlements, is something that concerns all interests, whether market, state or local community. The development of State of the Environment (SoE) reports, linked to the ongoing definition of environmental, social and economic thresholds in a coherent evaluation framework, could provide a real focus for the Local Agenda 21 process, and support for sensible decisions about future development.

Linking back to sustainable urban form

What, then, are the implications of environmental capacity assessments for the 'compact city' versus 'new settlements' debate. Earlier it was noted that *partial* assessments of capacity are currently being used inappropriately to shape decisions on settlements. The *comprehensive* framework discussed above, though as yet untried, would be a more appropriate approach for several reasons : first, because it takes into account the full recognised range of environmental stock, global to local (and potentially social and economic criteria too); second because it encourages the analysis and recording of environmental data as part of SoE reporting, rather than relying (as some of the current practice examples) on hunch and local politics; third, because it recognises that environmental factors can create development *potential* as well as development *constraints*; and finally because it obliges relative values and trade-offs between different factors to be made explicit.

When the comprehensive appraisal is applied to decisions about urban form and settlement pattern. There are likely to be certain general conclusions. Picking up the examples cited earlier, the countries such as Berkshire and Hampshire which used environmental capacity to safeguard rural resources would be obliged to take a more balanced view, recognising urban resources as well. What is more, a county such as Berkshire, which is part of a metropolitan area, not an island, would ideally be tackling appraisal in concert with neighbouring counties, so that the relative capacities are assessed across a functional region and appropriate allocations made. Integrated capacity studies could for example be orchestrated by SERPLAN. Failing that, the county has to accept its allocated share of housing as *given* and use the capacity analysis to distribute that share between settlements within the County.

The case of Chester could also be dramatically affected by redefining the area so as to include the commuting sub-region of the city, not merely the built-up area. As a trail-blazing study on capacity, Chester is excellent, but by its nature it has given the city special (and costly) treatment in a way that is not equitable from the intra- or inter-generational standpoint. The treatment could not be duplicated everywhere else. It is about particular functional and perceptual thresholds, *not* environmental capacity.

If a wider area were taken, and the 'global climate' capacity criteria were applied, the result would be challenging. Access to facilities, reducing the need to travel, would become central for residential development. Access to public transport nodes would become a key determinant of commercial location. Car-based edge of city retail parks would be deterred (in line with PPG6 but not with the recommendations of the Chester study). Conversely the logic for concentrating more residential development in and around Chester rather than in satellite towns might well be powerful. The green belt would be under threat, but for environmental reasons. Unless, that is, effective decentralisation of employment opportunities occurred, and the planners' ability to negotiate mixed use development increased.

The vital extra ingredient in this process is *accessibility*. The guide to Sustainable Settlements (Barton et al 1995) suggests a large number of specific thresholds for accessibility. For example, that 80% of new homes should be within 400 metres of local shops and primary schools and within 1500 metres of a district (or small town) centre.

The basis for such thresholds is proven in *general* (See, for example, ECOTEC 1993; and Farthing, Winter and Coombes 1994) but there is no doubt much room for argument over the *exact* levels. Such criteria put a premium on sites that are close knit into the urban fabric, and dismiss sporadic or 'out-on-a-limb' development.

Impact on the compact city principle

There are potentially two contrasting perspectives given by capacity studies on the principle of the compact city. In the first place a careful study of urban capacity (learning from the Chester exercise, but not replicating it) will show the degree to which intensification is or is not possible. Housing stock capacities, perhaps estimated at ward level, will often indicate the likelihood of further falls in density as household sized fall, unless the rate of 'wildcard' site releases, reclamation, and redevelopment at higher densities can compensate. The definition of urban green spaces as critical or constant environmental stock (highly used and/or valued) will guard against 'town cramming' and over-intensification, except in lower density leafy suburbs.

So, in so far as the compact city strategy relies on urban intensification, appraisal of environmental capacity will lead to an onset of realism, and the recognition that there are severe limits on the number of people who can be squeezed into existing urban area without sacrificing quality of life.

But, conversely, a study of accessibility thresholds will, as noted in the case of Chester, tend to reinforce the attractiveness of places where there are jobs and facilities, and the sites that are close in to centres of activity, at the expense of ex-urban or dispersed development. Towns and cities that have land around them within certain distances of the central area, close to existing or potential district centres, and well served by public transport would be favoured, presuming of course that the land is not defined as critical stock for reasons of (say) flooding, rare habitat or high landscape value.

So the principle of the compact city might well be reflected in continued suburban growth, based on public transport and pedestrian accessibility, rather than intensification.

Impact on the new settlements strategy

Using the thresholds tentatively suggested in Barton et al (1995) then the maximum accessible population (by foot) for a *single-centred* small town (or a district in a big city) would be 20 - 40,000, depending on shape and density. The normal *maximum* for a 'compact' city with a dominant city centre would be 200 -400,000 again depending on local geography. These maximum figures and the assumptions they are derived from demand further research, but at least give an indication of scale, and can be compared with other figures such as the 25,000 *minimum* for an antononous town suggested by the DoE (1994).

Achieving a fair degree of autonomy is critical to the validity of the decentralised 'new settlements' strategy. The question of exactly what catchment population triggers the provision of particular facilities (eg. superstore, leisure centre, railway station) is important but can be rather artificial because of the uniqueness of each town. Estimates of environmental capacity (with 'reducing the need to travel' incorporated) emphasise locations close to existing centres and facilities. So the capacity analysis will tend to have a conservative influence on settlement policy, reinforcing the status quo, and excluding dispersed solutions.

This points to an innate limitation of the concept of environmental capacity. Even at its most catholic (as recommended here) it takes a historic view. Essentially it reflects the state of the environment as it *is*, shaped by past events, rather than as it *could* be, shaped by dynamic forces of change. Barton et al (1995, p.69) emphasise that 'while assessment of environmental capacity is an adequate technique for project appraisal, it is not in itself sufficient for plan-making. Consideration of settlement form can provide a trigger for the more dynamic, integrated and creative thinking that is necessary.'

It would be possible, though, to use capacity analysis more imaginatively, as a means of evaluating the impact of possible new growth points: eg. *If* a new mixed use centre could be established at a particular location, then how would that alter the environmental capacity? Thus creative ideas for the evolution of the land use/movement system are complimented by a systematic approach to environmental impact appraisal.

Conclusions

Earlier we examined the way in which the concept of environmental capacity is currently being used. The conclusions were alarming. The notion of 'Capacity' is often being used by particular interests as a development stopper, and far from promoting sustainable development, may in some instances be reinforcing unsustainability. The problems stem from (i) the perverse confusion between environmental carrying capacity and local community impact; (ii) the absence, with some notable exceptions, of any proper analysis of capacities; (iii) the false assumptions that capacities are fixed, rather than being thresholds which can be overcome by changed management regimes or extra investment; (iv) the highly selective range of environmental criteria that are often employed. It was noted that decisions on settlement patterns and urban form are being distorted by all these factors.

The recommendation, taking a cue from the guide to Sustainable Settlements, is that analysis of environmental capacity should necessary be taken to encompass *all* the elements of environmental stock. The technique that is suggested is a conceptual framework that encourages the comprehensive view, using the checklist of 'global to local' elements of environmental stock from the good practice guide to Environmental Appraisal of Development Plans. The framework encourages the creative management of capacity levels where appropriate, by distinguishing *grades* of constraint. It deals with the positive environmental benefits of development (regeneration, accessibility) as well as the problems raised. And it tries to differentiate between matters of fact and/or 'professional' judgement, and matters of value and 'political' judgement. What it does not reflect adequately at present

93

are economic and social questions of commercial viability, community impact.

Applying this comprehensive and systematic approach to the current debate over sustainable urban form, the conclusions are:

- The ideal of the compact city, implying a reliance on urban regeneration and intensification, is not realistic in many cases because of the falling capacity of the existing housing stock and the importance of protecting urban environmental capital, especially open spaces.
- The brave new world portrayed by advocates of new/expanded 'rural' settlements could have undesirable impacts on global climate unless or until a high degree of local autonomy can be realistically achieved.
- The practical and environmentally sound alternative to compact cities or new settlements is suburban growth, but the precise nature of that suburban growth is critical to success.
- Any suburban growth should be closely tied in to existing development and town/district centres, based around public transport accessibility and pedestrian access, but respecting sites of critical or constant environmental capital.
- Effective environmental capacity analysis is a necessary part of planning. It could usefully be extended to include key social and economic criteria so that it becomes a tool in planning not just the environment, but sustainable development.
- The environmental capacity framework provides a useful tool for project and plan appraisal. It is not, though, primarily a prescriptive exercise (though helps define the limits of prescription) and is not adequate by itself to the task of plan-making. It needs to be complemented by other, more creative, policy-making processes.
- The framework for plan appraisal also is the framework for environmental monitoring. New information and policies can be incorporated so that ongoing appraisal of development projects becomes a simpler task. Each proposal is effectively subject to a simple EIA. And development interests, keen in being ahead of the game and ensuring a smooth side of their proposals, can pay for site-based information. Community groups at the same time can access environmental information and contribute to its updating.
- Thus the varied environmental data and decision process become closely interconnected. Site based information is organised and given meaning by the environmental capacity framework. The SoE reports, project appraisals and plan appraisals are all sourced from the same place. The process necessarily involves other departments as well as planning, and can help to enfranchise the wider community.

Notes

1   Downs, Sally (October 1995) - Environmental appraisal lecture at UWE, Bristol.

References

Bannister, D. (1992), 'Energy Use, Transport and Settlement Patterns' in Breheny (ed) *Sustainable Development and Urban Form*, Pion: London.

Barton, H (1994) 'Environmental Appraisal and Environmental Capacities' Paper given at the RSPB's Second National Planners' Conference, Nottingham 24 Feb. 1994.

Barton, H., Davis, G. and Guise, R. (1995), *Sustainable Settlements : a guide for planners, designers and developers*, University of the West of England and Local Government Management Board, available from the Research Secretary, Faculty of the Built Environment, UWE, Coldharbour Lane, Bristol BS16 1QY.

Breheny, M. (1992) 'The Contradictions of the Compact City Form : a Review' in Breheny M. (ed.), *Sustainable Development and Urban Form,* Pion: London.

Buchanan, C. (1963), *Traffic in Towns*, HMSO: London.

Cheshire County Council, Chester City Council, DoE, English Heritage and Building Design Partnerships (1994), *Chester: The Future of an Historic City* Cheshire CC, Chester CC, EH.

Commission of the European Communities (1990), *Green Paper on the Urban Environment*, (COM/90/218) EC: Luxembourg.

Countryside Commission (1993), *Position Statement: Sustainability and the English countryside*, Countryside Commission: Cheltenham.

Department of the Environment (1993), *The Environmental Appraisal of Development Plans; A Good Practice Guide*, HMSO: London.

Department of the Environment (1994), *PPG13: Transport*, HMSO: London.

Ecologist Magazine (1972), *Blueprint for Survival*, Jan edition, Whole issue, Vol 2, No 1, Ecosystems Ltd: London.

Ecotec Research and Consulting Ltd in association with Transport Planning Associates (1993) *Reducing Transport Emissions Through Land Use Planning*, HMSO: London.

Environmental Resources Management (1995), *Environmental Capital and the Countryside*, Countryside Commission: Cheltenham.

Farthing, S., Winter, J. and Coombes T. (1994) 'Reducing the need to travel through land-use planning policies: a study of facility provision on new residential developments' PTRC European Transport Conference, University of Warwick, pp. 105-116, PTRC: London.

Grigson, S. (1995), *The Limits of Environmental Capacity*, Barton Wilmore Partnerships and House Builders Federation: London.

Hillman, M. and Whalley, A. (1983), *Energy and Personal Travel: Obstacles to Conservation*, Policy Studies Institute: London.

Newman, P. and Kenworthy, J. (1989), 'Gasoline consumption and cities - a comparison of US cities with a global survey' *Journal of the American Planning Association*, Vol. 55, pp.24-37.

Ove Arup (1993), *Environmental Capacity and Development in Historical Cities: Methodology Report*, Cheshire CC, Chester CC, EH.

Sherlock, H. (1991), *Cities are Good for Us*, Harper Collins: London

Sidaway, R. (1994), 'Limits of Acceptable Change in Practice' *ECOS* Vol. 15, No. 2, pp. 93-107.

Stead, D. (1994), 'Three land use challenges for local planning authorities' in Farthing, S. (ed.) *Towards Sustainability Conference Papers* Faculty of the Built Environment WP38, pp. 33-40, University of the West of England: Bristol.

7 Community involvement in Local Agenda 21: the experience of Bristol City Council

Tessa Coombes
Martin Fodor

Introduction and background

Agenda 21 was drawn up at the Rio Earth Summit in 1992 (the United Nations Conference on the Environment and Development) as an agenda for the 21st century and a commitment to sustainable development: 'development which meets the needs of the present generation without compromising the needs of the future' (World Commission 1987). The Earth Summit concluded with a commitment from governments around the world, including the UK, to prepare national sustainable development plans.

Chapter 28 of Agenda 21 states that by the end of 1996 every local authority should have developed a Local Agenda 21 (LA21) through consultation with its citizens. Over two thirds of the actions required to make a sustainable development plan reality require the involvement of local government. Local authorities are being encouraged to initiate campaigns which help work towards more sustainable communities. These are being defined as participatory, local efforts to establish comprehensive action for sustainable development (LGMB 1993). Local authorities all over the world are starting to translate the global sustainability agenda into local action and the response in the UK is promising to be considerably higher than many countries. In the UK, Local Agenda 21 is defined as 'a process of building partnerships between local authorities and other sectors to implement and develop local policies for sustainable development' (Bateman 1995).

Agenda 21 and its implementation at the local level is therefore a truly global process, which is one of the things that makes it so innovative and exciting: hundreds of local authorities globally have made a strong commitment to the LA21 process (Whittaker 1995) and there are national campaigns in at least 7 countries so far (UK, Netherlands, Sweden, Japan, Australia, Denmark, Finland). Local government, according to Whittaker (1995), has been developing environmental policies and practices in response to a number of different national and international initiatives prompted by the Brundtland challenge of 1987 (Brundtland

1987). A much broader and more holistic approach is now called for.

The twin pillars of Local Agenda 21 are, according to the LGMB Step by Step Guide (1994):

- ensuring a move toward sustainability in all areas of development locally, which will require adoption of best practice in each field of activity;

- involving people from all walks of life, social groups and sectors; empowering women and minorities to take part in the process of preparing and implementing the plan.

The LA21 process is a non-statutory process, therefore there are many barriers to implementation: lack of funding, other more pressing priorities, a lack of awareness by councillors of sustainable development issues, and the traditional separation of issues by professions. One of the biggest problems, besides those described above, that all local authorities face in the implementation of a LA21 is how to motivate people, both within and external to the organisation. How do we make the issue of sustainability accessible and attractive to people and encourage them to play a part in the process; and is the local authority the right vehicle to lead the process? It is true to say that most local authorities have responded in a positive way to the challenge of LA21, but the contemporary restructuring of local service provision coupled to ongoing budgetary cuts has reduced their capacity to respond adequately to the demands of LA21. The response does need to be seen within this context in terms of what local authorities have managed to do despite the constraints.

Local authorities, as part of LA21, need to reassess their role and engage in policies and practices that allow participation by local people. The impact of such involvement depends upon local authorities having the power, competence and resources to act upon the results of such consultations and share decision making with community groups (Patterson and Theobald 1995, p.261).

Local authorities currently use a variety of techniques and mechanisms for consulting and involving the public, but are these adaptable to, or useful for, LA21? Or, is this a very different process that requires a different approach? Currently, according to a survey carried out by the University of Westminster, only a small number local authorities are vigorously progressing the communications dimension of LA21, using new techniques and mechanisms such as community profiling, targeted communications and making attempts to get representative LA21 fora and even fewer again are actually engaged in new consultative mechanisms as part of the process (Whittaker 1995). In terms of action, local authorities will have to make careful choices about what they can achieve in the short term and priorities will need to be guided by local circumstances, needs and opportunities (Levett 1994, p.207).

The advice to UK local government has identified six key areas for action to achieve these goals (LGMB 1994). These have been called the six steps in preparing a LA21 or local sustainable development plan:-

STEP 1   *Managing and improving the local authority's own environmental performance*

STEP 2   *Integrating sustainable development aims into the local authority's policies and practices*

STEP 3   *Awareness raising and education*

STEP 4   *Consulting and involving the general public*

STEP 5   *Partnerships*

STEP 6   *Measuring, monitoring and reporting on progress towards sustainability*

There does seem to be a definite tendency, at least initially, for local authorities to make progress on the 'easier' problems first and to tackle the first few steps of LA21 where control is greater, than the latter where reliance on, and partnership with, others is more important. The overall vision of what constitutes a sustainable city is much less developed as part of local authority policy and practice. Bristol City Council has undertaken substantial work already and has made considerable progress in some areas, in particular with steps 1, 2, 5 and 6 but further work is needed to develop best practice in steps 3 and 4 corporately, as illustrated by the following discussion.

The '6 steps' in Bristol

The circumstances for Bristol need to be seen in terms of its role as a regional capital confined within historic boundaries and the advent of unitary status which brings with it a wide range of changes and major challenges: how to manage commuter impact on the local environment; public health issues; keeping the city centre alive and vibrant.

The structures within the council for environmental policy making and implementation are not unusual. This includes the following: a cross directorate officer working group on green initiatives (GIWG); a corporate joint sub committee (GIJSC) comprising the chair/vice chairs of key service committees (Planning, Health and Environment, Personnel, Education, Leisure), reporting back to the Policy and Resources Committee; the corporate lead being taken by the directorate of Health and Environmental Services. The Council has a corporate commitment to the implementation of the Green Charter and 'Environment' features strongly as a core value of the authority.

The discussion that follows highlights current practice in Bristol in relation to the six steps of LA21 outlined by the LGMB (1994).

1.   Managing and improving the local authority's own environmental performance

The city council approved its Corporate Green Charter in 1990. This builds on specific policies and covers all major areas where a local authority needs to take action to influence the local environment:-

- energy conservation and resources
- purchasing power
- environmental quality control
- the built environment
- the natural environment
- movement and access

Eco Management and Audit (EMAS) was begun within the city after a reappraisal of its responsibilities and the need to implement its Green Charter. A council-wide environmental management system was initiated with assistance from CAG consultants. In late 1993 Bristol was one of the first authorities in the country to begin to put the EMAS regulation in place corporately. The direct effects of the organisation comprise one set of initiatives; the services of the council another. Each is being developed by a team from all responsible Directorates.

2.   Integrating sustainable development aims into the local authority's policies and activities

Since the launch of the Green Charter in 1991 the council has developed a corporate approach to implementation, with a corporate Green Charter annual action plan that has achieved national note - in particular for ensuring targets are set by all Directorates to achieve the necessary action (for more detail see Fodor, Speeden and Whittaker 1995, pp.27-29).

Other existing initiatives, complementing the green charter have demonstrated imaginative approaches to tackling the key sustainable development issues of energy inefficiency, wasted resources and biodiversity. The Bristol Energy and Environment Plan was launched in 1991 to tackle the city's demand for energy resources and over the last decade Avon Friends of the Earth and the Bristol Recycling Consortium have initiated a range of initiatives which are now being developed in partnership with the city council: kerb side collections, CFC recovery and business scrap recycling. Community waste reduction initiatives have also been encouraged. A Greater Bristol Nature Conservation Strategy has identified the key steps to protecting and securing important species and habitats in the area, working with various agencies and groups. It is now incorporated in the land use planning policies of the Bristol Local Plan.

3.   *Awareness raising and education*

The subject of environmental education and awareness raising is now receiving attention in the preparations for unitary status. The city council has developed the CREATE centre, recycling a disused tobacco warehouse to achieve a vision for partnership working and a focus for recycling, environmental action, public information and education. Numerous groups in the city now use CREATE for meetings, events, exhibitions, conferences and office space. The Avon Environmental Education Liaison Group have been very active in Bristol in working with existing voluntary sector networks and groups, including a series of training days in schools across the city and preparing local guidance on developing school grounds.

4.   *Consulting and involving the general public*

Participation in the governance of Bristol is one of the keys to a more sustainable city. A variety of consultation and involvement processes are already underway. The challenge is to ensure these embody the spirit of LA21. Some exercises relate to the redrafting of the Bristol Local Plan; schemes for neighbourhood renewal; the working of the council's Environmental Liaison Group; and a new partnership for the economic strategy. Also with the advent of local government reorganisation the council has had to take a closer look at how it consults with and involves the voluntary sector, as a result a major review has taken place of current practice with a view to proposing a coordinated corporate strategy for the whole of the new authority.

5.   *Partnerships*

Numerous partnerships are now in place, demonstrating the council's commitment to work together with both voluntary and private sectors in providing services to the city. Of particular note is the active involvement of officers and members in Bristol Environment and Energy Trust, which is a partnership of public, private, voluntary and academic players locally. For sustainability in the city to be achieved collaboration and new initiatives across the city and region are essential. The mission of BEET covers a range of actions and levels. Action groups have been set up to focus on waste, energy and biodiversity building on the initiatives described above. Other partnerships have included work on the Waste and Recycling Plan by the Recycling Consortium and the input of a number of local groups into the Nature Conservation Strategy. An annual Environment Festival celebrates and educates through events in the region. EnClub and the Greater Bristol Environmental Business Forum provide best practice guidance and information exchange for SME's and large companies.

Creating change in city neighbourhoods is a major priority for the council in Bristol involving the redirecting of diverse budgets to achieve significant improvements in the delivery of services and the quality of life in localities. A new Community Action Fund, to be managed and administered by BEET, has been set up by the council to support local action for sustainable development from many backgrounds and localities. The Choices for Bristol Project, being developed with Public Voice International and the support of many other agencies and organisations, has an important role in enabling people to make informed decisions about policies which determine future development and community conditions.

6.   Measuring, monitoring and reporting on progress towards responsibility

The publication of a State of the Local Environment Report has been a major step forward in measurement and reporting, including a series of ward-level indicators of sustainable development. This enables conditions in the city to be assessed as a basis for priorities to be set. The report has achieved a valuable reference for council and community use, but more importantly the beginning of a debate on priorities for local change. By introducing the ward-level indicators of sustainable development the process of community involvement in tackling local concerns has been initiated. Community involvement in local measurement is part of the process of involving the people of Bristol in shaping the future of local neighbourhoods.

The LA21 process in Bristol can thus be seen to be tackling all six aspects of the LGMB's principles and processes: corporate working; policy integration; public awareness; community involvement; partnerships and auditing. The key now is to ensure that the momentum is maintained and that awareness continues to be raised as widely as possible. The approach to involving the community is perhaps the most crucial aspect of a LA21 process and is one of the areas where many local authorities have been slow to take up the challenge.

The focus in the discussion that follows is on the community involvement process in Bristol. This needs to be seen within the context of some of the more academic and theoretical issues relating to community involvement and participation processes, which will act as background to the complexity of the issues being discussed and undertaken in Bristol. It is important to recognise these complexities as they have a dramatic effect on the success or otherwise of consultation and participation exercises undertaken with the local community.

Community involvement in LA21: the Bristol experience

LA21 is a process by which decisions are made in the community about the actions that are required to achieve sustainable development. There needs to be a commitment within the authority and the community to environmental improvements, enhancing the quality of life in a locality and a determination to find ways of integrating local groups and individuals in the decision making process, rather than purely concentrating on structural changes within the authority or imposing new developments on a neighbourhood in the name of regeneration and improvement.

A large proportion of local authorities are tackling many aspects of LA21, but what type of consultative processes are being used, how do they differ from existing practice and why is it important that they do differ? All groups in society must have a voice in deciding what sustainable development requires and in working towards it. There also needs to be some recognition of the complexity of local social life. There is not one community but many. Community is usually taken to refer to a particular set of relationships which occur in a specific geographical location. As has been frequently pointed out by sociologists, this idealised local 'way of life' hardly exists in contemporary Britain (Evans 1994). In most localities there is unlikely to be such a thing as a local community in any meaningful sense. Instead there are likely to be several, perhaps very many intertwined, overlapping sets or networks of social relationships which may touch but not interpenetrate to any great degree (Agyeman and Evans 1995).

This is perhaps the case in urban neighbourhoods, where social diversity may generate dynamic and vibrant local social networks, not based on geographical area but based on age, religion, ethnicity, class or race. In this sense there may be many 'communities', often with widely diverging expectations, hopes and values, but all sharing the same geographical area. Places may have meanings for individuals, but not all individuals will ascribe the same meaning to the same places. Certain social groups, usually the educated and articulate middle class or other well organised/mobilised groups, may have the capacity to create and dominate a local social world which can in turn exclude other less powerful groups. According to Agyeman and Evans (1995) this point raises serious doubts over the validity of any participation programme which does not take account of these complex social divisions and fractures which are likely to exist in any neighbourhood.

Any LA21 process needs to try and target under represented groups: women, youth, senior citizens, cultural/ethnic groups, disabled people, unemployed and economically disadvantaged. However according to a survey by Lancaster University (1995), the lack of trust in public officials and lack of a sense of agency is heightened amongst marginalised groups therefore more resources need to be allocated to such groups if their voices are to be heard. This is perhaps common in major planning decisions where recognition of change is realised very late in the day after statutory processes are concluded.

The constraints and issues highlighted above do have serious implications for the process of community involvement in LA21: there is no simple answer and no easy approach to this issue. Local authorities need to think more seriously about communities and their role in decision making.

The approach in Bristol, albeit in its early stages, has been directed by two key principles:

- the role of community led initiatives, and

- the importance of partnership working

These elements underlie the initiatives undertaken and are seen to be crucial to the development of a sustainable development plan for Bristol. The discussion that follows highlights the specific stages of the community involvement process and illustrates the main initiatives currently in progress.

In Bristol the approach has been led by the Green Initiatives Joint Sub Committee. As can be seen from the above discussion, the council has long been promoting environmental policy and practice in areas of its own work, for example, the Deposit Local Plan (1995) has a strong sustainability theme running through it as does the new Economic Development Strategy (1995) which places a great deal of importance on the balance between economic regeneration and environmental priorities: greening businesses and new green businesses.

A good deal of work has already been carried out into the environmental impact of the councils own operations: EMAS, Green Charter; and a State of the Local Environment Report (1995) to act as a starting point for consultation with communities about the most appropriate and relevant sustainability indicators for their local areas.

The approach to LA21 has been varied, with an initial particular focus on support for local community action through the identification, in the first instance, of a small fund to empower, enable and encourage local action for a greener, more livable city. There are countless local groups in the city involved in initiatives with an influence on local issues, to varying degrees and in various activities. The fund is provided to help these local groups to prepare plans identifying specific local problems and to develop strategies for action to solve problems. The fund is being administered by Bristol Environment and Energy Trust in partnership with the local authority, a kind of hands off approach in an attempt to reduce the bureaucracy of the process and also to lend support to the development of BEET, an important private, public and voluntary sector initiative, active throughout the West to encourage sustainable development.

As a kick start to this process of community action a workshop was organised during the Environment Festival by BEET, groups in the CREATE centre and UWE, in conjunction with the city council, to which 21 local groups were invited. 'Creating Change' was the theme of the day. Small group working with expert facilitators on hand to answer questions meant groups could discuss and tackle issues of importance to themselves.

The day involved community groups from across the city, and can be seen as the first in a series of workshops and seminars involving groups and asking them to set the agenda. The day was a great success with all groups working together and feeling very positive throughout the day. The feedback was largely positive with groups agreeing that further such workshops would be beneficial. One of the most rewarding elements was the way in which the day was organised to go beyond the usual participation exercises held by the council and actually engaged in debate and discussion with local groups with very positive ideas about where they thought

Workshop matrix issues, visions and strategies

	Poor quality of natural environment	Wildlife habitat loss	Poor quality of built environment	Poor use of waste land	Poor land use within development	Environmental awareness	Community involvement in planning	Pollution from industry	Graffiti and vandalism	Crime and security	Litter/dumping/dog fouling	Transport issues	Community services/facilities	Facilities for young	Unemployment	Noise	Affordable housing
Detail/examples																	
1 — What are we doing to affect environmental change?																	
How are we influencing others to affect environmental change?																	
2 — What could we do to affect environmental change?																	
How could we influence others to affect environmental change?																	
3 — What are our community objectives?																	

Figure 7.1 Creating change through community involvement

improvements could be made to their local environments. This actually got behind what people do or do not like about the area they live in and began to identify where responsibilities lie for improving problem areas without apportioning blame. For once, the council was not seen as the enemy or the provider of all things, there was a clear recognition that all sectors needed to be involved in LA21. It also demonstrated that environmental improvements are not an issue in isolation from other pressing concerns: local employment, social issues, safety, community facilities. Sustainable development links all these things together, as illustrated by the workshop matrix developed from the ideas and issues raised by the groups involved in the creating change day - see figure 7.1.

It is intended to run further workshops for different groups and organisations. One suggestion being developed at the moment is the idea of a youth agenda 21. Part of the approach in Bristol has also been to provide training for members and officers on sustainability and around the topics addressed to date in the Eco Management and Audit Scheme (EMAS).

The community involvement element of LA21 is now being led by a BEET Steering Group involving people from all sectors working together towards the same aims. This is what LA21 means, it is not about a local authority taking control of decision making, but is about sharing that responsibility. Having said that, local authorities are central to the process as enablers: they do hold key budgets and have a clear decision making role together with the administrative support needed to make LA21 effective. It is important therefore that local authorities take the opportunities being offered by LA21 and use this process as a mechanism to seek more innovative and positive ways of working with local people and communities.

It is important to seek public debate about what types of environment (social, physical and infrastructure services) the public want and their reactions to limitations on personal behaviour that may be necessary if limits exist to what is possible. A good example of this type of approach is seen in 'planning for real' exercises. A strategy for the future cannot however be constructed without analysing what the present situation is and what has occurred in the past.

One way, in particular, that this has been followed up in Bristol is through the 'Choices for Bristol' project run by Public Voice International with the support of the city council and other organisations. This project will develop and implement a new and innovative approach for helping the general public work out what kind of future they would like to see for their city and community, and what they can do to steer their community towards such a future. The project will act to strengthen local communities and inform key decision making processes in the public, private and community sectors.

The aims of the project, as stated by the Director of Public Voice, are to:-

- involve over 2,000 adults and young people across the city in discussions and problem solving on the future of Bristol and its communities

- produce results which aid decision makers and strategic planning in the public, private and community sectors
- provide a model for other communities throughout Britain to follow

The 'Choices for Bristol Project' translates the importance attached to involvement and empowerment of local people into practice by aiming to achieve a consensus on priorities and the way forward within our communities by the end of 1996. LA21 stresses the point that individual local action plans are needed (a key element of the work undertaken by Public Voice International) which include the following information and serve the functions outlined:-

- systematic identification, by means of extensive public consultation of problems/constraints and their causes
- prioritisation of tasks to address problems and limits
- creation of a vision for a sustainable community - give a sense of direction
- long term local action plan with measurable targets to implement best practice and achieve change

The above discussion serves to highlight the need for more effective forms of public consultation which broaden the participation base and enable local communities to have an input into policy formulation. Traditional methods, where members of the public are invited to submit comments on published documents, may fail to reach social groups who are less articulate, confident or familiar with bureaucratic processes. Again and again it is common to find consultation exercises record the responses of the 'usual groups'. Community empowerment is an important aspect of social sustainability and can change the situation/syndrome.

The concept of shared responsibility is also of key importance to the LA21 process: sustainable development requires a much more broadly based and active involvement of all economic players including public authorities, public and private enterprise in all its forms, and, above all, the general public, both as citizens and consumers. There is the need to seek a balance between the short term benefit to individual persons and longer term benefits to society as a whole of change and development.

To date 182 authorities have adapted or created new public consultation procedures to respond to LA21. Preliminary results from a recent questionnaire to local authority environment coordinators suggest that two thirds of local authorities in the UK are already undertaking LA21 work (LGMB 1995), but it is less clear to what extent this is just a continuation of existing environmental practice and how much is new and innovative working geared specifically to the needs of the LA21 process. Bristol is attempting to take on board the opportunities offered by LA21 and to embrace new ways of working by enabling residents to advise the experts and politicians, rather than merely continuing and extending current practice.

The lessons that have been derived from the experience so far in Bristol are discussed in the next section.

Lessons

- Local authorities need to think about who leads LA21 and how this can be done. It is important that there is a clear steer from the local authority in partnership with other groups to establish mechanisms and ideas/initiatives for LA21.

- A clear structure is needed within the local authority to deal with LA21 - a separate unit, LA21 officer etc. Clear lines of responsibility are needed and a first point of contact for all those involved in LA21.

- LA21 is a corporate process. It should not be seen as the preserve of one directorate, be that planning or environmental services. All the practices of the local authority need to be looked at in relation to LA21. All directorates need to be involved. Planning is only one of the areas where there is an obvious clear link with LA21: health, youth service, wildlife conservation, education, traffic and transport, etc, all matter.

- To be effective LA21 needs to be part of a corporate strategy which is able to carry the underlying principles of sustainable development into the policy processes across the authority. There is the need for a truly corporate approach, with clear links to, for example, development planning, community development work, health promotion, and the leisure strategy.

- Community involvement needs to be at the heart of the drive towards sustainable goals and objectives. An engaged, directed and mobilised community is an asset and a strength. Partnership and active communities need to underlie LA21 initiatives.

Conclusions

Despite the fact that the LA21 process is non-statutory most local authorities have a moral commitment to developing a sustainable development plan for their authority area. This brings with it the need to identify resources. There needs to be a bigger commitment from central government to the process of achieving sustainable development, backed up by adequate resources so local authorities can fund initiatives at the local level.

LA21 is a process by which decisions are made in the community about the actions that are required to achieve sustainable development. There needs to be a commitment within the authority and the community to environmental improvement and a determination to find ways of integrating local groups and individuals into the decision making process. It may also be necessary to make appropriate structural changes within the authority to deal with the LA21 process, but local authorities should not see their response purely in structural terms, this change needs to be responsive to the needs and requirements of the local communities and routine approaches and processes need to be reviewed and adapted

There is a good deal going on in the UK in relation to LA21, which should be applauded and welcomed. However, this is only the beginnings of a much bigger process which demands clear and democratic practices to be embraced by local authorities. The experience in Bristol suggests that communities are geared up to accepting the challenge that LA21 provides and can indeed take a lead role in the process. It is up to local authorities and business and industry to recognise this and utilise this extremely valuable resource to its full, the resource of local communities themselves and all they have to offer.

References

Agyeman, J. and Evans, B. (1995), 'Sustainability and democracy: community participation in local agenda 21', *Local Government Policy Making*, Vol.22 No.2, pp.35-40.

Bateman, D. (1995), 'Local Agenda 21 UK', *Local Government Policy Making*, Vol.22 No.2, pp.16-20.

United Nations Conference on Environment and Development (1993), *Earth Summit Agenda 21: the United Nations Programme of Action from Rio*, United Nations Department of Public Information: New York.

Evans, B. (1994), 'Planning and the chimera of community', *Town and Country Planning*, Vol.63, No.4, pp.106-108.

Fodor, M., Speeden S. and Whittaker S. (1995), 'Fostering a corporate approach to Local Agenda 21: using performance review', *Local Government Policy Making*, Vol.22 No.2, pp.21-29.

Hewitt, N. (1995), *European Local Agenda 21 Planning Guide*, ICLEI: London.

Lancaster University (1995), *Public Perceptions and Sustainability in Lancashire*, CSEC: Lancaster.

Levett, R. (1994), 'Options for a menu', *Town and Country Planning*, July/August, pp.206-207.

Local Government Management Board (1995), *Local Agenda 21 Round Table Guidance*, Nos.1-10, LGMB: Luton.

Local Government Management Board (1994), *Step by Step Guide - LA21, Principles and Process*, LGMB: Luton.

Local Government Management Board (1993), *Framework for Local Sustainability*, LGMB: Luton.

Patterson, A. and Theobald, K. (1995) 'Reorganising away the chance of success?' *Town and Country Planning*, October, pp.260-261.

United Nations Association (1995), *Towards Local Sustainability - A Review of Current Policy on Local Agenda 21 in the UK*, UNA.

Whittaker, S. (1995), 'Local Agenda 21 and local authorities', *Local Government Policy Making*, Vol.22 No.2, pp.3-11.

World Commission on Environment and Development (1987), *Our Common Future - The Brundtland Report*, Oxford University Press: Oxford.

8 Public opinion and environmental policy: the case of land use planning

Tony Harrison

Introduction

In 1989 the Planning for Social Change Unit of the Henley Centre stated in its Annual Report (Henley Centre 1989) that environmental concerns had overtaken more traditional worries (such as those about the threat of nuclear war) in the rank order of issues troubling the British public (see Table 8.1). This was in the same year as a single issue political party (the 'Greens') gained an unprecedented 15% of the popular British vote in elections to the European parliament. It also appeared that increasing numbers of individuals were modifying their own purchasing and waste disposal behaviour in the direction of 'environmental friendliness' (Elkington and Hailes 1988). These events could be interpreted as indicating that in terms of public opinion the time was ideal for shifting public policy sharply in a 'green' or environmentalist direction.

Those who had been arguing for some time that the western lifestyle, with its emphasis on material consumption and personal mobility, with associated profligacy in energy consumption and pollution generation, could be excused for thinking that their time had come. At last - or so it seemed - the public showed signs of being convinced that current modes of production and consumption were simply not sustainable if the interests of future generations were to be protected.

In fact, of course, things are not this simple. Widespread concern about an issue does not indicate consensus on what should be done about it. It says nothing about the extent to which individuals will be willing to accept personal inconvenience or costs in return for the achievement of an apparently higher social goal. The fact that public show signs of being worried about a problem is no guarantee of agreement on its causes. And even if there agreement on all these points, this would not translate simply into a consensus about what should be done. The philosophical adage that 'you can't logically derive an ought from an is' as true in relation to environmental policy as it is in any other field.

111

Table 8.1
Major worries of a sample of people in Great Britain,
April/June 1989

1. Ozone depletion
2. Poverty
3. Cruelty to animals
4. Pollution of rivers and seas
5. Threat of nuclear war
6. Inner city problems
7. Nuclear power

Source; Planning for Social Change 1989/90 Programme; The Henley Centre.

But the fact that converting public opinion into policy raises difficult problems does not mean that public opinion is unimportant. It is argued in this paper that a basic precondition in a democracy for the successful implementation of any environmental policy is public acceptance of its legitimacy. But this is only one precondition - it is necessary but not sufficient. This raises three fundamental questions about environmental policy. These are;

1. What environmental *'outcomes'* does the public apparently want? Some may be relatively simple and non contentious - though difficult to achieve - (clean air, protection from potentially harmful short wave radiation, stabilisation of climate so as to halt sea level rises and desertification may be some of these), but others raise more difficult problems. Amongst these may be local environmental outcomes in which personal taste and values play a larger role (the mix of new and old buildings, the provision of public space, landscape etc).

2. What *trade offs* are regarded as acceptable in achieving or moving towards these ends? The nature of environmental policy is such that short term costs are an almost inevitably part of the price that has to be paid for longer term benefits. These are bound to impact on personal behaviour - they may limit what some see as 'freedom' to use the private car (or at least change the personal cost of so doing), they may change the availability and price of consumer products that have become standard features of daily life, and they are almost bound to limit in some way what an owner or occupier of real estate can do with that property. In other words, the fact that costs will fall on all or some (and almost certainly do so unevenly across different social groups) will mean that recognition that these costs are worth suffering to achieve higher benefits is crucial.

3. What *means* are regarded as acceptable ways of setting objectives for the

outcome of environmental policy, and of making decisions about the weight to give to different considerations when they appear to be in conflict? In a democracy these means must be political, but the more specific question here concerns the *institutional arrangements* through which political decisions are reached. It is argued here that unless both the arrangements and the manner in which they are used are widely accepted, then any environmental policy emanating from then will lack legitimacy and lack the consent needed for its successful implementation.

These three questions are examined here in relation to one area of public policy in Britain, land use (or in the terms used in British legislation, Town and Country) planning . This is selected for a number of reason. First, it is one of the key areas of policy identified by the United Kingdom government through which environmental policy - and particularly policy directed at 'sustainability' - is to be implemented. Secondly, most environmental problems (energy consumption and generation, land, water and air pollution, human induced environmental disasters such as floods and severe soil erosion, and loss of valued landscapes for example) can be traced back to the ways in which land is used. Consequently, patterns of land use are central to addressing environmental problems at all scales from local to global. Third a recent study of public attitudes to land use planning allows some conclusions to be drawn to the three questions identified above. This survey related to the structure and procedures of a system with specific institutional features, so it will be necessary to outline the salient characteristics of that system. However, first a conception what environmental policy and the policy making process means in the context of this paper is discussed.

Local environmental policy and the policy making process

Defining environmental policy presents formidable problems. At its limits any facet of human behaviour - and so any aspect of public policy - can be said to have an impact on the environment. However, an all embracing definition in which environmental policy is seen as everything has no analytical capabilities; if it is everything, then it is nothing. For the purpose of analysing the problems of environmental policy it is necessary to try to specify any characteristics that distinguish it from other areas of policy.

It is suggested here that there are two important elements to a definition of environmental policy. The first concerns those features of the world that policy aims to influence - the objects of intervention. The second is the means by which policy seeks to bring about those changes.

A convenient starting point for defining the object of environmental policy is to see it as concerned with environmental goods, the benefits of which are consumed by people not as a result of a market based processes of choice in which proprietorial rights are transferred from one party to another, but simply as a result of membership of society. In other words an ideal definition of environmental goods is to see them as common property resources from which people cannot be excluded (Brown and Jackson, 1990). They are not, however, pure public goods in the economic sense because they do not exhibit the characteristic of non rivalness. Once used beyond certain levels of intensity - for harvest and production or for waste disposal - one person's consumption is rival to that of another because the resource is degraded. More specifically in the context of discussions about sustainable development one generation's consumption is rival to that of those that follow. This, of course is the common explanation for the environmental crisis, and is tellingly illustrated in Hardin's 'Tragedy of the Commons' (Hardin 1977).

But there is a distinction to be drawn between environmental goods that exist at different geographical scales. The public concerns noted at the start of this paper were largely about global environmental goods. These have specific characteristics and raise very particular problems of policy in that they appear to require heroic levels of international cooperation. Global environmental goods would appear to differ from local environmental goods in three clear ways.

First, the benefits of their existence are highly diffuse. Global oxygen, an ozone layer in the upper atmosphere and a stable climate and sea levels are potentially enjoyed by all (though, of course, other conditions may severely impede the ability of some so to do). Secondly, these are not produced by human agency. Human action is relevant to the existence of global environmental goods as a result of its capacity to destroy or detract from their quality, or to bring about conditions that allow natural processes to start their repair. But the actual mechanisms that create global environmental goods are 'natural'. Thirdly, the costs of reclamation and repair of global environmental goods may reduce the material standards of consumption of some or of prevent others from reaching those standards. These costs will fall on different people at different times. The first to 'suffer' are likely to be those about to 'enjoy' high material standards; the later will be those who aspire to such standards but whose immediate prospects of reaching them are remote. This, of course, makes the politics of global environmental policy enormously problematic and fraught with accusations of short term self interest, greed, envy and shortsightedness.

Local environmental goods have a number of features that distinguish them from the global category. First, and obviously, the fact that they are local means that the benefits of their existence are available to a more limited area - though the fact of their being 'environmental' means that within this area their availability is collective. Secondly, because local environmental goods include things like landscape and townscape, human agency enters as a producer as well as a detractor. Thirdly, because the provision and maintenance of local environmental goods tends to be so closely related to land use (and land is often privately owned), then the costs of repair and provision tend to fall on more specific shoulders. Fourth, the costs of damage can in some cases be 'exported' in different forms to other localities (as visual intrusion or acid rain for example). Fifth, (and this is particularly important in the politics of local environmental policy), some local environmental goods can be 'claimed' by the economically and politically powerful as a result of their ownership of land to become their own 'positional' goods (Hirsch 1977). An example of this is the benefits to existing residential property owners of Green Belt controls over further development - though it should be noted that these controls may generate very high costs to some land and property owners as a result of their inability to gain from the increases in land values that follow from permissions to develop.

These distinctions between global and local environmental goods are summarised in Figure 8.1. There are clearly links between these different scales (demonstrated in the 'think global act local!' slogan), and there are obviously intermediate scales between global and local (eg continental regions) where the defining characteristics start to break down. However, it is argued that this distinction clarifies the subject of this paper which is about attitudes to an aspect of *local* environmental policy.

If environmental goods (the object of policy) have certain distinguishing features, this is far less true of the processes by which environmental policy is derived and implemented. These political processes are clearly not unique to environmental policy. However, it is argued here that environmental issues impact on political process in particular ways. This is illustrated by a simplified model of the policy process that is described below and illustrated graphically in Figure 2. For convenience the policy process is divided into a number of stages, starting with public awareness of an issue and concern that 'something should be done about it', and finishing with the implementation of policy that in turn influences public perceptions.

Public concerns about environmental matters are potentially triggered by a wide range of influences. One is direct experience (most likely in relation to the local environment where changes impact on the senses in the most prominent way, and where the attribution of cause is most obvious). Catastrophes (floods, radiation emissions from nuclear power stations, oil spills) are another, but here it is most likely that for many experience is mediated by news reports, and in some cases the perception of cause is dependent upon scientific interpretation. The dissemination of scientific findings which report environmental changes that may be barely perceptible, yet which cause alarm, and which attribute these changes to human action are another potential trigger.

Awareness of an issue is not a sufficient condition for there to be political pressure on the part of the public for action by those holding power. It is possible that either concern is not sufficiently great to overcome the personal costs of action, or that the public view the political system with such cynicism that action is not considered worthwhile -a negative response on the part of those in power is anticipated. Such non action feeds back to environmental outcomes as 'no change'. Unless politics is seen as a game played for its own sake, a precondition for action is a belief that an appropriate response from the political system is likely.

DECREASING GEOGRAPHICAL SCALE > ------- > ------- > ------- > ------- >

GLOBAL ENVIRONMENTAL GOODS	LOCAL ENVIRONMENTAL GOODS
* benefits are highly diffuse (eg global oxygen, ozone etc) * no 'primary' human producers (human agency either consumes within environmental capacities for reproduction, or depletes, or attempts to repair) * costs of reclamation and repair potentially fall on all, but at different times. May generate conflict between the materially advantaged and the poor who aspire to improved material conditions in the future. This may take the form of conflict between different global regions.	* benefits diffuse though within more limited area * human agency acts as both a producer (eg countryside, built environment), and detractor * costs of repair and provision tend to be specific * costs of damage can be 'exported' in many different forms (eg acid rain) * can be 'claimed' by economically and politically powerful, and become 'positional goods' (eg properties in environmentally protected areas)

Figure 8.1 Global and local environmental goods

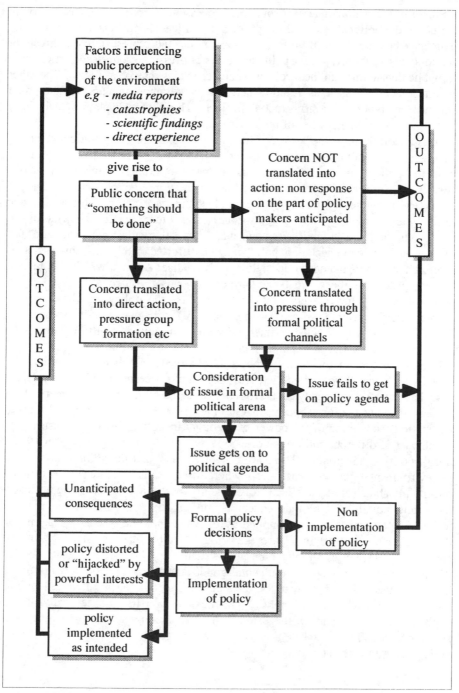

Figure 8.2 A simplified model of the environmental policy process

Pressure for action may take one of two essential routes. One is to try to influence the political system through formal political channels and public debate. This may take the form of voting, pressure on elected representatives, threats of withdrawal of support, joining political parties or pressure groups and participation in public debate through the media or whatever means may be available. The other is direct action - such as is now increasingly common in opposition to road schemes and other major infrastructure projects. This obviously plays a particularly important part in the politics of the environment.

Pressure on those in the formal political arena (parliaments, local councils and their supporting advisory and administrative bodies) may or may not get an issue onto the policy agenda. If it does, and it leads to explicit policy changes two further possibilities arise. One is non implementation - action requires that the necessary resources of money, power and competence are put into place, and policy can obviously fail at this stage. The other is that the means of implementation are established. But even then, particular outcomes are not guaranteed. On implementation, policy may be distorted or 'hijacked' by particular interests, so that its intended effects do not materialise. Alternatively it may be that the complexity of the world being influenced leads to outcomes that were not anticipated by policy makers (or in other words, the policy was based on an inappropriate conception of cause and effect). A third (maybe unlikely) outcome is that policy is implemented as intended with the required results. Whatever the outcomes these feed back to public perceptions of the environment.

This conception of the policy process is obviously simplistic. It presents the process as being driven by public perceptions and concerns, and it is clearly the case that energy may equally come from the concerns of those 'inside' the political system. It shows the formal political system as separate from society , and it gives no explicit recognition of the power of ideology in influencing consciousness, of the impact of different political cultures on environmental policy (Crenson 1971), nor of political advertising. These are obviously very real possibilities in relation to environmental policy - particularly where discourse is beset by such enormous uncertainty about cause and effect. Consequently there will be many more feedback loops and possibilities of independent action in different parts of the process influencing outcomes than are implied by this account. The summary diagram of the process as outlined in Figure 8.2 should not be read as 'starting' at any particular point, but as an interconnected system.

The conception of local environmental goods and of the policy process outlined here provides a broad context for considering the relationship between public concerns and environmental policy. The next section looks specifically at the institutional arrangements of the British land use planning system, which, as was stated above, is one of the key means by which the government sees environmental policy being implemented.

British land use planning and environmental policy[1]

An important distinction needs to be drawn between the aims of the land use planning system and the means it has at its disposal in attempting to achieve these aims. The relative stability of the mechanisms and instruments available to British planning since its comprehensive introduction in 1947 are in contrast to the varying vigour with which these have been used in promoting different policy aims. These issues are reviewed in Healey (1992) and Healey and Shaw (1993).

The mechanisms and instruments of British land use planning rest on six key features which have been consistent elements of the system since 1947. These are;

1. The 'ownership' of the rights to develop land by the state, with a consequent requirement that in general any individual wishing to develop land requires permission to do so from the state (usually a local authority).

2. A legal definition of development which indicates what type of development requires planning permission. This definition is embodied in statute, and operationalised through a large body of case law where disputes over what does and does not count as development has gone to the courts. Not only new development, but also changes in use in general count as development and require permission. However,uses that lie in the same class, as specified in a Statutory Instrument known as the Use Classes Order, do not.

3. A specification of developments that can be carried out without the need to obtain planning permission. Some of these are general and relate particularly to relatively minor developments (like small extensions to dwelling houses) and some relate to particular uses (for example agriculture, or the operations of statutory undertakers). The main source for developments not requiring permission is a development order made by the Secretary of State for the Environment, and the most significant of these is another Statutory Instrument known as the General Development Order.

4. The considerations that will be taken into account in deciding whether or not planning permission should be granted in a particular case. The general term for these is 'material considerations'. These can cover a range of things, like the impact of a proposed development on interests of acknowledged importance, the extent to which a proposal is in line with central government policy, what the findings of an environmental impact statement indicate about the effects of the proposal, or, crucially, whether the development accords with policy for land use as set out in a Development Plan of the local authority concerned.

5. Arrangements for the enforcement of planning decisions. These include procedures through which authorities must go if they believe development has

119

taken place without or in contravention of a planning decision, and penalties that are available in the event of such an act being proved.

6. Procedures available to parties who feel aggrieved in one way or other by a planning decision. Two such sets of procedures are important. One is an appeal to the Planning Inspectorate (and ultimately the Secretary of State) on grounds of policy - in other words on the grounds that the various factors and considerations involved in reaching a decision have not been correctly weighed against each other. The other is an appeal to the Courts on legal grounds. What is at stake here is an argument that the law and the prescribed procedures have not been properly followed.

A number of comments of particular relevance to the use of the planning system for the implementation of environmental policy follow.

The first concerns the weight that environmental considerations will have in the making of any planning decision. This is not prescribed in law; planning decisions are based on judgements that in the case of significant proposals involve the weighing up of different factors against each other. Amongst these, environmental considerations have become increasingly important in recent years. Environmental Impact Assessments required by European law for certain types of development imply more systematic and rigorous examination of the environmental implications for these developments - and this seems to suggest giving them more weight.

Secondly, government policy itself also points to attaching greater weight to environmental considerations. Government guidance, which is a material consideration that must be given weight in decision making, is set out in a number of places, but one of the most important is in a series of Planning Policy Guidance Notes (PPGs). The significance of environmental considerations is illustrated in a number of these. For example, in the early part of PPG1, General Policy and Principles (DoE 1992a, para. 3) it is stated that:

The Government has made clear its intention to work towards ensuring that development and growth are sustainable. (...) The planning system, and the preparation of development plans in particular, can contribute to the objectives of ensuring that development and growth are sustainable. The sum total of decisions in the planning field, as elsewhere, should not deny future generations the best of today's environment.

Further, PPG12, Development Plans and Regional Planning Guidance (DoE 1992b, para. 6.1) says:

Local planning authorities have a key part to play in helping to achieve the vision for Britain and the environment in the 1990s (...). One major responsibility is to ensure that development plans are drawn up in such a way as to take environmental considerations comprehensively and consistently into account. In this way environmental improvement can be plan led, and individual development decisions taken against an overall strategic framework that reflects environmental priorities.

This guidance is followed through in other PPGs dealing with specific activities and land uses. For example, PPG6, Town Centres and Retail Developments (DoE 1993) states at its outset the role of the planning system in:

emphasising the role of existing centres and local shops, including village shops, in development patterns that minimise the need to travel and promote transport choices that help to keep down CO_2 and polluting emissions.

This is reinforced in PPG13, Transport (DoE 1994, para. 1.3) which says:

By planning land use and transport together in ways which enable people to carry out their everyday activities with less need to travel, local planning authorities can reduce reliance on the private car and make a significant contribution to the environmental goals set out in the Government's Sustainable Development Strategy.

A third factor of growing potential importance for environmental policy is the weight that is attached to the land use policies of a Development Plan. It may seem obvious that these should given particular weight when decisions about development proposals are being made. Historically, however, for a number of reasons, they were given no more weight than any other material considerations. Firstly, many local authorities did not produce site specific development plans for their areas. Secondly, in those cases where they had been produced the plans may have been made obsolete by social and technical changes not foreseen at the time of their preparation. Thirdly the British planning system rests on striking a balance between local and regional or national considerations, and in certain circumstances regional or national factors were judged to override local considerations. And finally, the British planning system is not one based on zoning, in which a decision can be read off from what a plan says about a particular site. It is based on discretion and the exercise of judgement, where different considerations are weighed against each other at the point when the merits of a particular proposal were being considered.

Such a system has some advantages. It is more flexible than a zoning system which has the danger of embodying the criteria of a specific time. These may be inappropriate to conditions which were unforseen at the time when the plan was devised, and may also fail to anticipate special factors that come into play with specific proposals in particular places. But the discretion and judgemental basis of the British system also led to enormous problems. It encouraged many appeals by applicants who had suffered refusals for planning permission, and this led to high costs and to increased uncertainty.

This situation led to a review of the role of development plans in the early 1990s that was embodied in S54A of the 1990 Town and Country Planning Act (inserted by the 1991 Planning and Compensation Act). This section potentially establishes a situation in which the development plan carries greater weight when decisions on planning applications are being made than other considerations. (In planning terminology it establishes the primacy of development plans). The key section of the legislation says

> where, in making any determination under the planning acts, regard is to be had to the development plan, the determination shall be in accordance with the plan *unless material considerations indicate otherwise*.(emphasis added).

In conjunction with a requirement that all local planning authorities prepare district wide development plans (or Unitary Development Plans in the case of metropolitan authorities), and with a strong emphasis on the plans reflecting a process of choice on the part of the local population, this new situation sets the scene for the possibility of the environmental aspirations of the people of a locality being embodied in the development plan, and of this having special status when particular proposals are being considered.

The potential significance of public opinion about the environment becomes crucial. If certain environmental outcomes are held to be important by local people and these are reflected in the relevant land use plan, if public support is maintained for decisions based on the principles set out in the plan and these remain in place even when challenged through appeals, then the conditions appear to be in place to allow the public to make 'big' choices about the environmental goods to which they want access.

There are, however, a number of demanding conditions to be satisfied for these events to materialise - and crucially each one of these must be met before the next comes into play. These are:

- firstly, there must be sufficient public support for particular environmental ends,

- secondly, if there is such support it must find a means of expression in a manner seen as legitimate by those wielding political power (and this demands that the public know how to do this),

- thirdly, the agreed plan must reflect these public preferences rather than those of other bodies whose aspirations may be different,

- fourthly, the plan has to be consistently applied and any major challenges to its provisions rejected, and

- finally, as the implementation of the plan proceeds so continued public support must be maintained.

These are demanding conditions, and nobody can foresee with confidence the extent to which they will be forthcoming over the 15 years or so of the implementation of a plan. However, the 'Attitudes to planning' study (McCarthy and Harrison 1995) provides one means by which the extent to which those conditions are currently in place can be assessed. It is to this that we now turn.

Attitudes to town and country planning

This study addressed three sets of questions to different sections of society. These were:

- first, people's perceptions and level of knowledge of what town and country planning is about,

- second, the extent to which people had direct contact with the planning system, and,

- third, people's aspirations for and judgements of land use planning as it is carried out in England and Wales.

The study did not enquire into or seek to comment on the validity of these judgements but simply attempted to find out what they were.

The attitudes of six different sections of the public were researched. The public as residents was divided into two groups: the 'general public' who had no recent direct experience of the planning system through the submission of a planning application, and the 'applicant public' who had such recent experience. A sample of each was selected using a stratified random sampling method designed to be representative of the population of England and Wales as a whole. The public was divided into these two sections to see whether recent contact with the system made much difference to knowledge about it, and to allow for an evaluation of direct contact with the system where people had experience of this.

The remaining four groups were businesses who had recently submitted planning applications, developers, landowners who had an interest in development in that they had recently made applications to develop, and non governmental organisations. The organisations from these groups were not strictly randomly chosen to be representative of the larger population of which they were part, but were selected for interview for the likelihood that their attitudes would be indicative of widely held views. The interviews with major developers, landowners and NGOs were, in effect, with 'key actors' in the planning system and provided considerable insight into how a large number of highly informed people saw the

123

planning system as working.

This discussion concentrates on the two aspects of the study seen as most relevant to using the land use planning system as a means of implementing local environmental policy. These are, firstly, the extent to which the general public know about and support the town and country planning as a means of intervention, and secondly the views of key actors about the implementation of environmental policies through land use planning policy.

Public knowledge of and support for planning

This section concentrates on findings from the household surveys (the general and applicant public). It is asserted that if a particular form of intervention is to be successfully used to implement environmental policy, then this must command public support and knowledge, and that this is particularly true where it impinges on what people may see as their right to do as they wish with their property.

The aspect of planning that impacts most directly and obviously on people is the need to obtain planning permission for development (development control). The evidence of the study is that the public in general know that there is such a system of control and have some knowledge of how this works.This knowledge is not uniform across all groups - young, non home owners and members of minority ethnic groups know less than that of older white home owners for example. But it suggests that since its introduction in 1947 the need to obtain planning permission for development has penetrated the public consciousness to such an extent that it is little questioned and that there is even a relatively high level of knowledge about what does and what does not require permission. If anything the public err on the side of caution in believing that some actions that do not actually require permission do so (14%, for example, believe that painting a house a bright colour requires permission).

Knowledge that permission is required is one thing; equally significant for the legitimacy with which planning is viewed is understanding of who makes decisions and on what basis. On this count the public is relatively ignorant. Only 25% of the public recognise local councillors as those with responsibility for making decisions on planning applications. Just under one third of respondents were unable to suggest anyone in response to a question about who makes planning decisions. But in spite of this there is a surprisingly high level of rudimentary knowledge about the factors considered (material considerations) when decisions are being made. Physical considerations that impact on the surroundings of a proposed development (eg kind, size and design of development) are ranked high compared with incorrect considerations such as the nature of an applicant or the cost of development.

Knowledge of the development control process is in sharp contrast to that about development plans - the documents that set out land use planning policies and guide physical development through a period of up to 15 years. Only about one third of the sample claim to have heard of development plans in general, and this drops sharply in relation to the more specific types of plan. Knowledge of who prepares plans is very low indeed (e.g. of those who recognised the term Structure Plan, only 11% knew that these were prepared by a county council). Low levels of understanding of the purpose of development plans is also evident. Similarly, only a third of those who recognised the term development plans could recall being given the opportunity to comment on one.

There is, then, a reasonable level of knowledge about the mechanism for controlling development, but a generally low level about the decision making process on development proposals, and on development plans. What then becomes significant is public views about the underlying purposes of planning control; what, in other words, do people believe control over development is trying to achieve ?

Public understandings of this were assessed in two ways. Firstly by simply asking people what they thought town and country planning was for, and secondly by asking people to rank what they perceived to be the aims of planning, and in contrast what they thought the aims should be. Answers to these give considerable insight into the extent of potential support for using the planning system as an instrument for implementing environmental policy.

The most common unprompted perceptions of what town and country planning is about (attempted by three quarters of the sample - most of whom suggested more than one purpose) are that it is concerned with the layout of the built environment (over one fifth of all responses) and with the preservation of the non built environment (15%). There is little of a contentious nature here, but, perhaps, a surprising level of general knowledge as to what planning is.

Perceptions of the purposes for which planning is actually used reveal some interesting contrasts with what people think the objectives of planning should be. From a list of 8 possible aims of planning (varying from ones that focus on development to others in which the emphasis is on the conservation of natural and built environments) the perception is that planning's main preoccupation is with the location of transport infrastructure (particularly roads). This is in sharp contrast with the view that this should rank bottom of the list. Conversely, protecting the countryside and creating a healthy environment are middle ranked in peoples perceptions of what planning does - but they are equal top in what they think it ought to do. However, the conservation of wild life and protection of attractive landscapes come low in the list - below job creation.

A similar analysis compared public perceptions of who had benefited from planning with their views of where the benefits should lie. Property developers are seen as those who have gained most, with others (such as businesses, the general public, individual householders,large landowners and professional groups) clustering below these. Unsurprisingly, in the list of where the benefits should lie the general public is clearly alone at the top of the list, followed by individual householders and businesses. All other groups cluster at the bottom.

Whilst accepting the limitations of an extensive survey that did not allow for in depth discussion with people as to what lay behind their views, some potentially interesting (though highly generalised) implications for environmental policy come from these simple findings.

First, people are willing to accept control over development (frequently citing the 'chaotic' consequences of none). They recognise the potential of such control for achieving 'higher' social goals like creating a more healthy environment, but believe that currently it is used for less important purposes such as road planning. They have very little understanding of the decision making process, and equally little of that by which longer term policies for the use of land in an area are devised.

In a democratic political system with complex institutional arrangements and ways of making decisions it may be that continued consent for ways of carrying out public policy, is based on impression, feel or 'gut reaction' to performance. Given this, responses to questions about the 'value' of planning in general, and of it in comparison with other public services are instructive. Only 10% of the general public feel planning to be of no value whilst over a half describe it as very valuable or valuable. However, when compared with a list of 10 other public services, ranging from those that provide direct services (e.g. the National Health System), to others that are protective (the fire service), redistributive (social security) and (like planning), regulatory (environmental health) in no case does planning show as being more important. It comes closest in the cases of environmental health and trading standards.

The implications of general public attitudes to planning for its use in implementing environmental policy are not, then, straight forward or simple. Valuing the existence of a system for controlling development, appreciating its potential for bringing about environmental improvements, and knowing something about the extent to which it limits the ability of individuals to alter their property or use their land as they wish is one thing. It is quite another to actually support the manner in which this system is used and to accept any personal costs or inconveniences when actual decisions are made. These are differences between support for something in principle, and in practice. The evidence from the DoE study is of considerable support for the principle of land use planning. But whether that support is sustained must depend ultimately on its perceived performance. Some insight into this issue can be gained by looking at the perception of major and regular users of the planning system of both its current performance and of how it is likely to respond to the pressures currently being placed on it. It is to these matters that we now turn.

Attitudes to planning of major direct 'users' of the system

The term 'major users' includes individuals and representatives of organisations from a variety of groups ranging from developers and land owners to non governmental organisations. It would be expected that the aspirations and expectations of these groups would vary - and to some extent they clearly do. However, the intention of this section is not to describe what those aspirations are but to use the insight gained from a series of interviews and the completion of questionnaires to assess two things. Firstly, how well the planning system is currently performing in their view, and secondly, whether, as a consequence, it is likely to command widespread support for the implementation of environmental policy.

This section is not presented as revealing a set of attitudes that are statistically representative of a wider population, and in this sense they have to be treated with care. What it does is to discuss the significance of a range of opinions that recurred on numerous occasions across the groups studied, and which give grounds for considerable doubt about whether planning as it is currently being practised can be expected to deliver the objectives of environmental sustainability expected by some.

The discussion is under four main headings; the variability of performance of different local planning authorities, extreme suspicion of the decision making process, the extent to which a particular interpretation of the environmental agenda is coming to dominate planning, and major reservations about the way in which S54A (the primacy of the development plan) is being implemented.

Performance of different local planning authorities The British planning system in principle gives considerable discretion to individual planning authorities - though successful appeals against refusal and increasingly strong central government planning policy guidance have arguably eroded this. This has combined with the distinctive political cultures associated with different local authorities to give rise to a perception of sharply contrasting performance of different planning authorities. This is in part reflected in the importance that they attach to different objectives (pro growth and job creation, for example, as opposed to being preservationist), but what is seen as more important is their attitude to negotiation, their accessibility and the transparency with which decisions are made.

It is on these criteria that authorities are seen to vary most. The perception is that 'bad' authorities are those where access to a competent and well informed officer is difficult, where a position is taken that suggests little or no scope for negotiation, and where there is a perception that the 'real' reasons for a particular decision is obscure. The perceived 'bad' authorities also take more time over decisions, frequently ask for more information (in association for example, with a environmental impact statement) and then appear not to use it in informing a decision, and encourage a generally adversarial approach to discussions. Such authorities are commonly seen not just as obstructive, but as lacking basic competence.

Good authorities contrast on all these points. Interestingly major planning decisions are seen as nothing other than political, but it is commonly asserted that the output of political decision making is far more acceptable where both the bureaucratic procedures that lie behind these are efficient and accessible, and where the decision making itself is seen as open.

The decision making process This leads to perceptions of the decision making process itself. At its best there is little complaint; members (political representatives) are seen as open, well informed, capable of delegating to officers all that is correctly left to them, and bringing a healthy degree of 'common sense' to decisions. However a common perception is that the nature of the planning system lends itself to being corrupted and misused for purposes other than planning. This is seen as resulting from two things; one is the impact of planning decisions on land and property values.

The other is the lack of clarity as to what is a 'planning matter' and therefore a legitimate consideration when decisions are being made. In the view of many this leads to a situation where decisions that are 'really' made for unacceptable 'political' reasons being justified in planning terms. Examples of this range from suspicions that refusals of permissions for open cast mining were 'really' more to do with political opposition to the privatisation of the coal industry than with their environmental impact, to assertions that a district's refusal for a proposed development from a county (under different political control) was a result of 'political spite' rather than a careful consideration of the planning merits of the case. It should be noted that these interviews were carried out shortly after a period considerable public concern about the propriety of planning decisions. This followed widespread publicity about decisions leading to 'sporadic development' in North Cornwall. These appeared to disregard government guidance and strategic policy for the area, and it was asserted that these may have made been for the personal benefit. The media coverage surrounding this may well have influenced respondents in this study.

Planning and environmental policy As was stated above the planning system in the United kingdom is seen by government as a key mechanism through which environmental policy is to be implemented. This intention comes from both UK government policy, such as in the White Paper 'This Common Inheritance'(UK Government 1990) and from European Union rules (such as those requiring environmental impact assessments in association with certain types of planning applications). These changes in policy and procedures have come at a time of greater expressed public concern about the environment.

Many of the major users of the planning system view the implementation of environmental policy through planning with deep concern, however. The story, as told by many, goes something like this. An overly strong preservationist bias is emerging, and this is increasingly justified with reference to the concept of *sustainability*, a term that has slipped into usage but which has quite different connotations from that of *sustainable development*. This, it is argued, plays to an articulate and well informed middle class constituency, more concerned to preserve private amenity than to ensure a high quality public environmental quality. In places it results in extreme difficulty in getting permissions for major developments that may generate jobs in manufacturing industries, produce new infrastructure, provide affordable housing on a large scale or allow for much needed new settlements. Though rarely actually preventing these, it places sufficient barriers in their place to slow development down, make it more expensive and, possibly, inhibit proposals from ever coming forward.

128

It uses procedures (such as consultations or requirements for additional impact studies) to slow down or delay decisions, and results in an inequitable distribution of costs and benefits between a generally well off middle class population and an increasingly marginalised and unemployed 'underclass'. This whole process is underpinned by three features of the planning system. One is its position in a system of local government that increasingly focuses on relatively small localities but is not counterbalanced by a real decision making capacity at strategic levels. The second is a system that historically focuses too much on control and gives insufficient power to the implementation of new policies (for example, for urban regeneration). The third is its impact on land and property values and its inability to instill sufficient confidence that any private losses in amenity would be adequately compensated by public gains.

The new 'plan led' system This, of course, is a characterisation of a somewhat extreme position. However, it resonates with sufficient opinion to be taken seriously. The implementation of the new 'plan led' system, it is argued by many, reinforces these tendencies. Though the reality may turn out to be different, many planning authorities are seen as practising an over zealous approach to plan making. Insufficient attention is given to requirements of flexibility; plans are 'loaded down' with protectionist policies, and the 'precautionary principle' is taken too far in that potential developments that are perceived as threatening local amenity are excluded in land designations before there is a careful evaluation of their costs and benefits.

Again, this is an extreme version of a particular view. It has to be set beside one which says this view is born of frustration at the delays in plan preparation that are inevitable given their potential significance to land owners and their determination to influence plan content. A learning phase in plan preparation is an essential part of a new system, and if decisions based on inflexible and inappropriate plans are challenged through appeal when applications come forward, they will succeed given that the plan remains but one material consideration (albeit one that has special status). In other words, this view holds that there are sufficient checks in the system to prevent the worst fears of those suspicious of the new system from being realised.

It can be seen in these views that the crux of whether the planning system can be used to implement environmental policy lies in its ability to make difficult decisions and to do so in a way that commands support. Whether those decisions be at the plan making or development control stage it is difficult to conceive of a situation in which they can always be carried forward on consensus. Some conflict between private and public loss and gain is structured into planning by the place specific nature of developments and their impact on neighbours, by its influence on land and property values, and by plain differences in personal preferences.

This discussion is concluded by going back to a question asked at the beginning and considering whether the planning system can satisfy the three conditions necessary for the implementation of environmental policy; provide clear signals about desired outcomes, provide an ability to weigh conflicting factors (trade offs) and provide a means of decisions making that commands support.

Environmental policy and planning

Planning and the desired outcomes of environmental policy

Results of the research reported here, and of other research, indicates a growing public concern that environmental issues should weigh more heavily when land use decisions are being made. Evidence quoted here shows aspirations such as protecting the countryside and creating a healthy environment score high in the rankings of the general public as to what the planning system should be doing, whereas concern with the location of transport infrastructure is ranked low. This simple conclusion may be read as lending weight to the environmentalists case. However, has to be modified with two reservation.

One is that it appears that the public does not look to the planning system for all aspects of environmental protection. Thus, conserving wildlife and protecting attractive landscapes came low in public rankings for desired objectives of planning. The interpretation of this finding is difficult - it is not clear whether this means that these are seen as being of limited importance in general, or whether it indicates that they are not seen as being the particular concern of planning (ie, wildlife conservation is seen as the responsibility of some other area of policy, or that within the remit of planning there are other objectives of greater significance). This raises the question of trade offs between objectives that is considered below.

The other reservation concerns the extent to which the planning system can be used to provide clear signals about public preferences (or choices) in relation to environmental outcomes. In this respect the evidence has to be that it cannot at present.

Broadly, preferences will be revealed in three ways; through the political system, through formal public consultation when land use policies are being put in place, or through direct action.

The extent to which the political system at the local level can deliver clear signals about preferences of the wider public has to be viewed with doubt. The evidence from the work cited here is that the public have very limited knowledge of the role of local councillors in the planning decision making process. Consequently it is difficult to see that aspirations could be directed at those who have formal responsibility for decision making, though it remains possible that public preferences will be articulated as a result of the sensitivity of political representatives to something termed the public will. The problem here, of course, as many have pointed out, that on many issues there is unlikely to be *a* public will (Kitchen 1991), and in these circumstances there is a clear danger that political representatives respond to their interpretation of it, or to the voices of those who speak loudest.

It was difficulties such as these that led to provisions for public participation in planning, and, in particular, in plan making. As has been stressed here, recent reforms in the planning system mean, in principle, that more weight is attached to land use policies as laid down in a plan, consequently signals about public preferences are crucial at the plan preparation stage. There is no doubt that many local planning authorities have made enormous efforts to involve the general public in plan making, and have developed imaginative and innovative approaches to doing this. In spite of this, the evidence is that general public's knowledge of development plans, and of their opportunities to influence their content, is extremely limited. Once again, then, the conclusion is that the planning system appears not to provide a mechanism through which clear signals about public preferences for the ways in which land is used. As is so frequently the case, the danger is that the development plan system provides opportunities for some voices to be heard, and for those to weigh disproportionately in actual policies.

Planning and the weighing of conflicting considerations

Wherever conflicts exist decision making involves weighing or trading off different considerations against each other. This is obviously a common requirement in relation to most major, (and some minor), planning issues. So, a planning application to extend an airport may require that the potential costs of noise, congestion on local surface transport systems, loss of undeveloped land and maybe of pre existing buildings are traded off against advantages associated with improvements in air transport services, local economic growth associated with the airport and so on. And in so far as these are the real costs and benefits they accrue to different people whose interests are in conflict, at different times. Many of the potential beneficiaries and losers may not yet be born, consequently decisions are being made on behalf of future generations. This is the nub of the 'sustainability' issue, and unless a planning system is capable of accommodating such complex issues its potential for implementing environmental policy is extremely limited.

Typically the conflicts in planning issues are presented as involving trade offs between short and long term gains, between the interests of economy as opposed to environment, between groups of people whose values vary, between local people and a wider population, and between the interests of present and future generations. Obviously resolving such conflicts involves political decisions - and the extent to which the planning system provides an appropriate framework for political decision making is considered next - but the issue considered here is that of whether the planning system can provide guidance to decision makers about public attitudes to making such trade offs.

The answer to this has to be that currently its ability to do so is very limited. Major trade offs are confronted at two stages; when policies are being laid down in development plans and when decisions about specific applications are made. Public views about trade offs at the policy making (particularly plan making) stage will only surface when knowledge about opportunities for involvement is high, and

131

when concern about emerging decisions prompts people to use their voice. The evidence from the study discussed here is that neither of these two conditions are met at present.

Moreover, there is suspicion that when large numbers of people do express views about a particular issue through, for example, formal submissions to local planning authorities, these may be the product of the orchestration by powerful and sophisticated pressure groups of all those who happen to feel a particular way. In these circumstances some feel that the response of decision makers may be more influenced by the numbers of people expressing particular views than by a careful weighing up of merits of a particular proposal against others.

It is more likely that voices will be heard when the need arises for decisions on specific proposals. These impact directly on local interests and consequently focus attention on the issues. But even here signals from the public about how conflicting factors should be weighed will not be clear. The greater likelihood of articulate middle class opinion being voiced, together with the greater propensity for those adversely affected to express a view than potential beneficiaries (who may not even be individually identifiable) make any attempt to weigh the overall impact of a decision in proportion to identified support or opposition fraught with difficulties.

These political problems enhance the importance of advice to politicians about the costs and benefits of particular courses of action. This raises questions about the relationship between politicians and their officers, and about the ability of the latter to give 'neutral' advice that attempts simply to outline the likely consequences of decisions. Two comments are relevant here. One points to growing scepticism on the part of regular users of the planning system about the extent to which planning officers feel free to give advice to their political masters - particularly about any trade offs between environment and the economy. Many assert, for example, that increasingly members influence the scope of environmental appraisals and of any investigations into the wider economic and social impact of decisions. The other indicates the sheer complexity of forecasting the consequences of different actions and the scepticism with which attempts to measure potential outcomes will be met.

But there is another more general trade off associated with the costs of state intervention and regulation of private action. This is between allowing the users of property to do what they wish with it, and the state exercising some control over such unrestrained freedom - with all that this implies for costs associated with slowing down decision making and administration. The resolution of this trade off at any one time is enshrined in planning law (which will say, for example, what sort of developments will and will not require planning permission), though the actual drawing of the line will vary from time to time according to the philosophy of the government of the day.

The evidence of the public attitudes study indicates that this trade off is recognised. Moreover, in general, some costs associated with curtailing the freedom of individual property owners, delay and the necessary public administration appear to be accepted as costs worth paying for some form of public control. This is particularly true in the case of residents (in the applicant survey of the attitudes study only 45% agreed with a statement that planning made decisions quickly, but only 28% felt that such delays were unnecessary), but it is even true of development interests. Thus, in the case of landowners only 4% agreed that it made decisions quickly, but 35% disagree with the proposition that this delay is unnecessary. When people are asked open questions about whether they value planning, and if so why, then repeatedly the answer is either that they do (or that they reserve judgement), and that the reasons for this go back to the wider costs of no control over property development.

The evidence of this study, then, suggests that the principle of control for the purposes of some wider good are generally accepted, but this does not extend to confidence that conflicting considerations can be satisfactorily traded off against each other under current planning procedures. Once again the principle of planning is accepted, but the practice is questioned.

Planning and decision making

The true test of the ability of the planning system to 'deliver' environmental policy in line with public aspirations depends on public confidence about the integrity with which difficult political decisions are made. In this respect it is difficult to separate the impact of attitudes about the conduct of public life in general from those about the practice of planning - the former clearly have such a strong impact on the latter. An attempt is made here to see whether there are any particular features of the planning system that may serve to erode public confidence.

Such features can be grouped into two categories. First come those that are structured into the planning system; those that are there however different planning authorities go about their work. Second, are those which arise from the way in which the system is used; these are features that people may come to associate with the planning system, but which could be different if the culture of the provision of the service were to change.

In certain respects conflicts of interest are structured into the very nature of planning. At the simplest level these stem from the place specific nature of physical developments and the fact that there will always be cases where some in a locality stand to gain and others lose from permissions for new developments either being given or withheld. This is a feature of any planning system. It is, however, arguable that these conflicts take on a particularly sharp from in Britain as a result of the impact of planning on land values and the very considerable gains landowners may stand to make when planning permission is given, or lose when it is withheld. This feature of British planning has been much discussed elsewhere (see for example Ambrose 1986) and will not be discussed here. However it is certainly arguable that this, plus the problematic nature of compensation arrangements for any loss of amenity suffered by private interests when locally intrusive developments are proposed, creates a context of conflict that can only be reinforced by the geographical facts of population density and crowding in Britain.

In these circumstances the manner in which the planning system attempts to mediate between interests will be crucial in influencing peoples willingness to accept outcomes that may be contrary to their own interests. In this respect the constant claim of those interviewees in the DoE research who had regular contact with the planning system that it has strong adversarial features that reinforced a 'win or lose' feeling about contact with it must be taken seriously.

Precisely why the planning system is seen in these terms must be a matter of some speculation. However people's comments give a number of strong clues. These are particularly relevant to the issue of environmental policy where the crucial decisions will be on major developments with significant environmental impact.

One concerns the actual nature of the planning service in a locality. This refers to its accessibility, the approachability of officers, the openness with which issues are discussed, the extent to which those approaching an authority feel that an issue is negotiable, the availability of information (including is costs), the extent to which 'technical' advice from officers is separated from political decision making by officers and the actual decision making process is open to scrutiny. Many factors go together to influence how an authority is seen, but the evidence of regular users of the planning system is of enormous variability across planning authorities in these respects, and of a similar variation in willingness to accept outcomes that may diverge from private interests.

A second perception is that the focus of the planning system is on decisions about tangible proposals in specific places, rather than a wider search for the best site for a facility or for other ways of solving a problem. In these circumstances, it is argued, people will use whatever power and influence they have to defend their own interests. Some claim that an element of personal loss is easier to accept where affected parties are convinced that what is proposed has been clearly demonstrated as being the best solution to a problem. It is, however equally clear that it would be naive to imagine that this rationalist view of public policy points to ways of solving fundamental conflicts over major issues such as road and nuclear power station construction. It is also evident that whatever may be said about the desire for a more comprehensive and rational approach to problem solving, minds are most focused where tangible proposals are being considered. Views are far more likely to be articulated then, rather than at an earlier stage when strategic policy is being discussed. The continuing problems of public participation in plan making and the low levels of public knowledge about development plans is evidence of this.

However, the real problem of the land use planning system when it comes to making difficult decisions is one which stems from its legal basis but may be reinforced by the manner in which the system comes to be used. This concerns what is seen as a 'planning matter'. It is quite clear that however hard governments may try to separate planning matters from others that are seen as more correctly resolved through some mechanism (within the private sector through competition, or in a different part of the public sector, for example) the public just do not see land use questions like this. Separating out decisions about energy policy from a land use decision about the siting of a wind farm; decisions about health policy from one about the conversion and redevelopment of a redundant hospital, or decisions about retail competition from one about the siting of individual hypermarkets just does not appear to make sense to a public likely to be directly influenced by these decisions[2]. In these circumstances it is not surprising that members of the public are frustrated by an apparent unwillingness of the system to hear and weigh their concerns, or that members of planning committees look for ways of justifying decisions made on non planning grounds in planning terms.

Conclusion

These issues serve to reinforce what is now part of the conventional wisdom; planning is a political activity which cannot be separated from the wider context in which it operates. This includes a complex of factors ranging from public attitudes and expectations about planning itself to wider questions of willingness of different interests to accept some personal loss for wider public gains, the regard with which political activity in general is held and the strength of views about particular issues.

Currently it would appear that enough people hold very strong views about environmental matters, and combine these with particular definitions of what constitutes acceptable environmental policy, to place enormous strains on a system that is charged with balancing different interests. This paper has argued that whilst the public expect the planning system to 'deliver' environmental policy, and that it is uniquely positioned to do so by virtue of its very nature, the wider conditions that would allow this to happen in a less confrontational (and more efficient) way are not in place.

Some conflict arising from land use decisions is inevitable. But without changes (for which there are no easy solutions) in the practice of planning, in aspects of its legal basis, in the willingness of more people to concern themselves with land use matters before they directly impinge on their own self interests, and, above all else, in the extent to which public life is dominated by relatively short term self interest, then the implementation of environmental policy incorporating principles of sustainability through the planning system faces a future of long and intense battles.

Notes

1 The research referred to in the second part of this paper was carried out by Prism Research and the University of the West of England, Bristol, for the Department of the Environment's Planning Research Programme. That research is published as *Attitudes to Town and Country Planning* (by Peter McCarthy and Tony Harrison), HMSO 1995. Any opinions and judgements

appearing in this paper are entirely those of the author, and do not necessarily represent those of the Department of the Environment, Prism Research or the University of the West of England.

2   These issues are discussed more fully in the case study section of the above research report.

References

Ambrose, P. (1986), *Whatever happened to planning?* Methuen: London.

Brown, C.V. and Jackson, P.M. (1990), *Public sector economics* (4th ed) Blackwell: Oxford.

Crenson M. (1971), *The unpolitics of air pollution* Johns Hopkins Press: Baltimore

Department of the Environment. Welsh Office (1992a) *Planning Policy Guidance: General Policy and Principles*. HMSO: London.

Department of the Environment. Welsh Office (1992b) *Planning Policy Guidance: Development Plans and Regional Planning Guidance*. HMSO: London.

Department of the Environment. Welsh Office (1993) *Planning Policy Guidance: Town Centres and Retail Development*. HMSO: London.

Department of the Environment. Welsh Office (1994) *Planning Policy Guidance: Transport*. HMSO: London.

Elkington, J. and Hailes J. (1988), *The green consumer guide* Victor Golancz: London.

Hardin, G. (1977), 'The tragedy of the commons' in Hardin G. and Baden J. (eds) *Managing the Commons*. W.H. Freeman & Co: New York.

Healey, P. (1992), 'The reorganisation of the state and market in planning' *Urban Studies*, Vol. 29, pp. 411-434.

Healey, P. and Shaw, T. (1993), 'Planners, plans and sustainable development' *Regional Studies*, Vol. 27, pp. 769 - 776.

Henley Centre Planning for Social Change Unit (1989) *1989/90 Programme* Henley Centre: Henley.

Hirsch, Fred (1977) *Social limits to growth* Routledge and Kegan Paul: London.

Kitchen, T. (1991) 'A client-based view of the planning service' in Thomas, H. and Healey, P.(eds) *Dilemmas of Planning Practice. Ethics, Legitimacy and the Validation of Knowledge* Avebury Technical: Aldershot.

McCarthy, P. and Harrison, A.R. (1995), *Attitudes to Town and Country Planning* HMSO: London.

UK Government (1990), *This Common Inheritance* CM1200, HMSO: London.

9 Bus based park and ride: towards sustainability?

Geoff Mills

In recent years park and ride schemes, particularly bus based, have been gaining in popularity as a means to combat urban congestion and provide environmental benefits. However, there has been a largely unquestioning acceptance that park and ride is environmentally beneficial and should form a significant element of a sustainable transport strategy for most towns and cities. This chapter considers the published literature and reports the results of a case study undertaken by the author on the Brislington park and ride scheme in Bristol.[1]

What is park and ride?

Park and ride involves the use of a private motor vehicle (usually from home) to an interchange where the vehicle is parked and the next stage of the journey is taken by public transport. On the return, public transport is taken to the interchange from where the car is used for the final stage of the journey. The public transport service can be provided by either rail, rapid transit or bus, but the focus here is on bus based schemes. In the case of bus based schemes the interchange is typically located at or near the edge of the town/city served.

Development of park and ride

Park and ride is not a new concept, the practice of driving from home to a railway station and then transferring to a train service has been a feature of travelling to the central areas of larger UK cities, especially London, for many years. Bus based schemes first developed in the late 1960s when a number of local authorities introduced Christmas services to cater for the additional demand for road and, more importantly, parking space at peak times (usually Saturdays).

The success (measured in terms of patronage) of many of the seasonal schemes led some 15 local authorities to attempt to operate them throughout the year, although only four in Leeds, Leicester, Nottingham and Oxford, attempted all day services catering for both commuters and shoppers. However, lack of use outside the pre Christmas period and mounting financial losses meant that of the all year schemes, by 1981, only Oxford and a much reduced operation in Nottingham remained. For nearly ten years the Oxford scheme was the only comprehensive bus based operation in the country (Bixby 1991).

Continuing high levels of traffic growth during the 1980s, coupled with increased awareness about the environmental effects of road traffic resulted in renewed interest in the potential of bus park and ride. During the mid to late 1980's there was a steady increase in the number of towns and cities opening all year Monday to Saturday schemes. By 1993, when the Bristol scheme opened, there were a total of sixteen operating year round on a six day week basis. In addition some 25 towns and cities were operating seasonal or Saturday only schemes.

Policy framework

In the early days park and ride was largely considered to be a way of meeting peak parking demand and as such was a component of parking policy rather than part of an overall transport strategy. However, in Oxford, park and ride has been an integral part of the city's transport strategy from the outset. This has involved expanding public transport, restraining 'unnecessary' car use through parking controls and improving conditions for pedestrians and cyclists. Park and Ride's position as an important component within a wider strategy is, Bixby (1991) believes, probably the reason why it kept going while others were failing.

The difficulties encountered by a number of the early schemes, particularly those that attempted to cater for commuters, resulted in many of the 'second wave' towns and cities taking a cautious approach. Their schemes were often initially directed at shoppers and visitors, particularly at peak times such as Christmas (ADC 1992). While at the outset, such schemes have tended to be stand alone, as patronage has developed they have been incorporated into an integrated transport policy. Shrewsbury (Shropshire C C 1994) is an example of this cautious approach but which now includes park and ride as an integral part of a comprehensive transport strategy. A more limited number of towns and cities including Exeter and Maidstone, having seen the apparent success of park and ride in cities such as Oxford, missed out the 'experimental' Christmas and Saturdays only stage. They have also opted to follow the Oxford example by including park and ride as part of their wider transport strategies and operating six days a week services from the outset (Bixby 1991).

Typically these strategies have sought to retain and improve the environmental quality of the town/city whilst supporting its economic development, particularly the economic health of its central area in the face of competition from peripheral developments. They therefore seek to reduce the amount of traffic entering the city through the development of networks of park and ride sites on or close to ring roads with frequent services between the sites and the city centre. Other complementary policies include priorities to assist both park and ride and local bus services as well as cyclists, and a range of parking restraint measures. These may include the restriction of new city centre parking provision, pricing existing provision at above that of the park and ride service, transferring long stay spaces to short stay, and residents only parking schemes.

The situation today is therefore one where, for many towns and small cities, bus park and ride is seen as a central component of transport policy. A policy which seeks to improve the urban environment by reducing car traffic whilst retaining the attractiveness of the central areas, and thus their economic well being, to shoppers and visitors.

Measuring success

The steady expansion of park and ride during the last ten years clearly indicates that many local authorities consider it to be successful, either in its own right or as part of a wider transport strategy, but is it contributing to the achievement of a sustainable transport system and how is its contribution being assessed?

Rigby and Jones (1991) consider York's scheme to be a 'dramatic success' on the basis that 330,000 passengers and 130,000 cars used the scheme in 1990/91 and the public subsidy is 'very low'. Likewise Rivers and Casement (1992) speak of the success of the Canterbury scheme in terms of 173,599 vehicles using the park and ride site and 325,113 passenger being carried in the first year of operation.

Day (1992) in discussing Exeter's traffic and parking plan considers park and ride to be probably the most effective measure brought in by the Plan. He cites usage and the fact that the operation of the service does not require public subsidy. Richardson (1994) considers the first two Norwich sites to be successful for a variety of reasons relating to the quality and price of the service and also due to the level of usage.

Centro (1992, px) have undertaken some research into not only the usage of the Coventry scheme but also user attitudes, origins and previous travel mode. They conclude that 'Overall, the survey highlights that the Coventry Park and Ride has succeeded in its primary objective - that of reducing traffic congestion within the central area of Coventry - as prior to the introduction of the service over three quarters of users made the same journey by car.'

The English Historic Towns Forum (1993, px) have no doubt that 'Park and Ride can make a significant contribution towards the alleviation of the adverse environmental effects of road traffic'. They do, however, consider that 'It cannot be the sole solution to these problems, and will need to be developed in conjunction with other transport policies for there to be a large environmental gain'. Although they refer to the success of many of the schemes provided in the historic towns and cities, the criteria against which this success is measured is not defined.

Pullen and Silcock (1991) examined the impact of park and ride at light rail stations in Newcastle. They found that, in the absence of the park and ride facilities, 47 per cent of users would have travelled to the city centre by car and 48 per cent by other public transport modes, principally bus. Applying these figures to patronage data resulted in a reduction in traffic flows to the city centre of between 1.7 per cent and 2.4 per cent, in the order of one year's car traffic growth. Pullen and Silcock concluded that their work reinforced earlier evidence from Tyne and Wear that park and ride has had little impact on car traffic flows into the city centre. To be an effective tool in relieving congestion they suggested other measures also needed to be undertaken such as restricting the availability of city centre car parking.

The most thoroughly researched scheme to date has been that of Oxford and it is worth considering this in some detail. In 1975 the Transport Studies Unit (TSU) at Oxford University undertook a study (Papoulias and Heggie 1976) to identify among other things the impact of the service in reducing traffic levels within Oxford. The study was undertaken on the Botley Road site which had opened seven months earlier. The study found that 43 per cent of weekday users and 32 per cent of Saturday users would either have undertaken informal park and ride or used the other park and ride site then in existence. This coupled with the fairly low level of usage (230 cars on a weekday and 250 on Saturday) relative to the frequency of the bus service (73 return journeys) led the study to conclude that, except in the weekday morning peak, the service was counter productive in terms of reducing the impact of traffic.

However, when considering the scheme after a longer period of operation other commentators have come to a different conclusion. Jones (1989) considers that '..park and ride has clearly been one of the most successful elements of the (Balanced Transport) policy.' He cites the four fold increase in use between 1975 and 1986 and the fact that in 1989 there was still no sign of growth abating. 'The key lesson here is that it takes considerable time for the use of park and ride to build up to significant levels..' He considers that the scheme has produced environmental benefits. This is because 'Assuming that provision would otherwise have had to be made for the vehicles using the sites in the city centre (or else they might have gone elsewhere), then public parking spaces would need to be increased by about 40 per cent and peak traffic flows on the busier corridors would be over 20 per cent higher.'

Bixby (1991) also used patronage as the main indicator of success or failure, pointing to the steady increase in usage. He considered it impossible to evaluate the effects of the Oxford scheme as it was part of an integrated package of measures but suggested that as the overall performance of a range of indicators was positive, it must therefore be making a positive contribution. Indicators cited for the period 1973 and 1986 were; motor vehicles entering the city fell by 2.4 per cent, central area parking provision declined by 601 spaces whilst retail floor space increased by 15.5 per cent and office floor space increased by 10.9 per cent.

Oxford City Council (1991) have no doubts that park and ride is a 'remarkable success' in environmental terms with, in 1992, 3600 cars entering the four sites on a typical weekday and 4500 on a typical Saturday. They quote abstraction rates from traffic flows on roads passing the sites as proof of this. Like Jones, Newson (1994) estimates that, assuming adequate road capacity and central area parking spaces, in the absence of the scheme there would be an increase in inbound traffic between 0800 and 0900 of 17.8 per cent, and over the 12 hour period 0700 to 1900 it would increase by 7.2 per cent.

Nevertheless, as the research of Papoulias and Heggie (1976) has shown, one cannot assume that all users would have driven into the city centre. A survey undertaken in October 1988 by Oxford Polytechnic (Newson 1994) at the Pear Tree site suggests that some 29 per cent of users would have otherwise travelled by public transport for the whole of their journey and a further 8 per cent would not have made the trip at all. This suggests that the scheme may have resulted in an increase in car traffic outside the city and that the net environmental impact would depend on the amount of car usage saved within the city.

More recently Parkhurst at TSU (Parkhurst 1994) has undertaken further research on the impact of bus park and ride. Users of the Oxford and York schemes were asked how they would have made their journey if the park and ride had not been provided. Although there are some variations in alternative travel behaviour on Saturdays, over a six day week there is a strong similarity between both cities. The proportion who said they would travel by car is very close at 57 per cent (Oxford) and 58 per cent (York). Similarly 10 per cent and 11 per cent respectively said they would not have made the journey that day or travelled elsewhere, and 24 per cent and 21 per cent would otherwise have used conventional bus. Parkhurst's survey results are broadly consistent with those of the Oxford Polytechnic survey described above.

Concerning environmental impact, Parkhurst (1994, p.?) concludes that 'Providing park and ride services are well used, they improve the space efficiency of the urban transport system in the area within the park and ride provision, and this is the area usually most seriously affected by congestion.' But he also considers that 'There is a need to consider the region as a whole, including the impact on traffic growth, trip generation and attraction, residential location and switching from modes other than the car.'

It would appear that most operators and promoters have equated the success of park and ride, judged in both economic and environmental terms, with usage. Put simply, the greater the usage the greater the success. Although some negative environmental aspects have been acknowledged, largely due to the provision of the car parks themselves, each car using the site is usually equated as one less car on the town or city streets.

Papoulias and Heggie (1976) drew attention to the situation that at low levels of usage there could be traffic and environmental disbenefits if the impact of the bus was greater than that of the cars they were replacing. They also drew attention to a fact seemingly ignored by many operators and promoters, that not all the users would otherwise have driven to the city centre. The work in Newcastle by Pullen and Silcock (1991), the Oxford Polytechnic survey (Newson 1994) and the recent study by Parkhurst (1994) of the Oxford and York schemes, have all shown that a substantial minority of users would have used public transport or other non car modes in the absence of the scheme. The existence of a substantial level of abstraction from non car modes must significantly reduce the apparent environmental benefits of a scheme and raise questions about the impact upstream of the sites, i.e. in the area outside the town/city served.

Although some of these studies have raised doubts about the actual level of environmental benefit to be derived from park and ride little attempt has been made to quantify this. The remainder of this chapter describes a study, undertaken by the author, which sought to identify the change in car usage brought about by the Bristol scheme. Identifying this change is important as the level of car usage is closely related to its environmental impact. If park and ride is to contribute to environmental sustainability then it will be necessary to show reductions in car usage and fuel consumed and thus in exhaust emissions, noise levels and visual intrusion.

Park and ride in Bristol

Background

At the end of the 1980s, growing concern about the impact of increasing levels of car use led Avon County Council to review its transport strategy for the Bristol area. The apparent success of bus based park and ride schemes elsewhere in the country, including that within the County at Bath, suggested that the potential of bus park and ride for Bristol should be examined.

A preliminary report (Avon CC 1990) indicated that there was sufficient potential demand, and journey time savings to be realised through bus priority measures, to warrant the provision of a pilot scheme serving the south eastern approach to the city. However, it did draw attention to the possibility of abstraction from existing public transport services on the Bath/Bristol corridor, particularly at Keynsham railway station, and to a possible increase in traffic flows on roads leading to the park and ride site. It also concluded that bus park and ride needed to be accompanied by bus priority measures and traffic restraint. Following this report the County Council resolved to prepare detailed proposals for a scheme. The Council also agreed that the development of a strategy for further park and ride schemes should be examined as part of the Bristol Integrated Transport and Environmental Study (BRITES) (MVA 1991) which it was about to commission.

BRITES supported the decision to pursue a scheme, serving the A4 Bath Road, based on a site located on the edge of the built up area at Brislington (see Figure 9.1). It went on to conclude that this scheme, together with three others (bus or

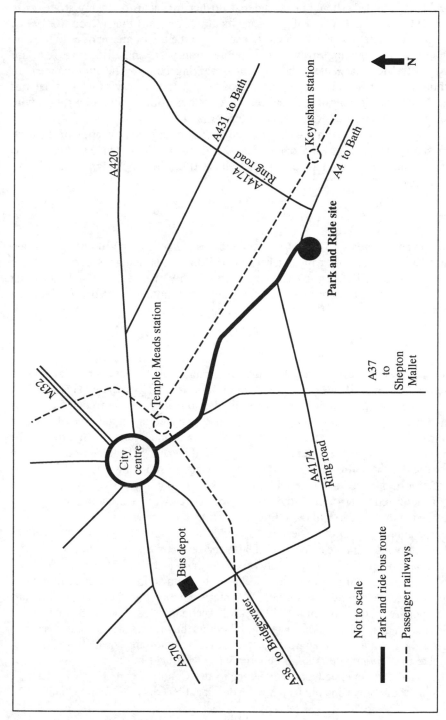

Figure 9.1 Location of Brislington park and ride, Bristol

rapid transit served) should be considered further for inclusion in any strategy. In early 1993 the County Council published its draft Transport Plan (Avon CC 1993). This set out a strategy which sought to encourage the use of alternatives to the car, principally through improvements to public transport, and discourage car use through traffic management measures and parking policy. The improvement of public transport included, over the period to 2003, the provision of seven bus based park and ride sites at or near the intersections of the main radial routes with the yet to be completed Ring Road around Bristol.

Work on the Brislington site commenced shortly after the publication of the draft Transport Plan and it was opened on 25 October 1993. On Saturdays it is supplemented by two temporary sites located on the northern and western approaches to the city.

The site

This covers an area of 5.5ha (13 acres) and has a capacity of 1300 cars. It is laid out to a high standard with extensive perimeter landscaping. Security features include powerful lighting, closed circuit TV (CCTV) surveillance and patrolling security guards. Passenger shelters and public telephones are also provided (see Photos 8.1 and 8.2). Total cost of the scheme was £2.8m.

The services

The service operates Monday to Saturday throughout the year. On Mondays to Fridays the hours of operation are 0700 to 1900 (to 2015 on Thursdays which is Bristol's late night shopping day). The Monday to Friday service frequency varies between every 7/8 minutes and every 12 minutes depending on the time of day. On Thursdays, the service after 1900 is at 20 minute intervals. On Saturdays, the service frequency is 12 minutes throughout the day. Scheduled journey time between the site and Broadmead, the main city centre shopping area, is 16 minutes in the morning peak and 14 minutes off peak.

The adult return bus fare at the time of the survey was £1.20 with accompanied children up to 15 years old travelling free. Multi-journey tickets for 10 return trips were available for £5.00. There is no charge for parking at the site. These fares were below those on the conventional bus services between Brislington and the city centre and below the train fare between Keynsham and Bristol Temple Meads.

New 76 seat purpose-built double decker buses painted in a distinctive livery and logo are used to provide the service. The buses comply with the Disabled Persons Transport Advisory Committee's (DIPTAC) recommended standards. They are of a higher standard than found on the city's other bus routes with features such as tinted glass and a public address system. Five vehicles are normally required to operate the service with a sixth undergoing service/held in reserve.

The service is operated under contract to the County Council by City Line, a subsidiary of Badgerline plc who are the dominant bus operator in the County. The

Photograph   9.1   The Brislington site parking area

Photograph 9.2 The park and ride bus at the Brislington site

145

vehicles are owned by City Line and operate from the company's Winterstoke Road Depot in the south west of the city.

The route

Buses travel between the site and the city centre via the A4 Bath Road, a distance of 4.25km. There then follows a 3km anti-clockwise route around the Inner Circuit Road (see Photo 8.3). There are four city centre stops serving the principal shopping, commercial, tourist and entertainment areas.

Existing sections of bus lane totalling 0.7km around the Inner Circuit Road are utilised together with lengths totalling 2.5km inbound and 0.6km outbound on the A4. The sections on the A4 were created specifically in association with the park and ride service but are also used in whole or part by a total of 13 other services (see Photo 8.4).

Avon County Council surveys (1994) have shown that the bus lanes on the A4 have reduced average Monday to Friday morning peak period (0700 to 0900) bus journey times from the site to Temple Meads by 42.7% (from 21.1 min to 12.1 min). Due to the more limited provision in the outbound direction the reduction in outbound journey times in the afternoon are smaller. In the afternoon peak period (1600 to 1800) they have reduced by 14.9% (from 13.4 to 11.4 minutes). The reliability of services has also improved as the variability of the journey times has considerably reduced. It has not been possible to assess the impact of the lanes on journey times for cars because of the opening of two major new roads which have had the effect of increasing traffic flows on some parts of the A4 whilst decreasing them others. For this reason it has also been impossible to identify the changes to traffic flows brought about by the park and ride services.

Survey of Bristol park and ride users

A questionnaire survey was undertaken by Avon County Council in March 1994, on a Wednesday to collect Monday to Friday data, and on a Saturday when trip purposes are likely to be different. The survey was designed to enable the County Council to improve the planning, operation and marketing of this and future schemes. However, in themselves the questions did not provide sufficient information to enable the change in car use to be estimated. The Council were therefore asked, and agreed, to include a number of additional questions that would facilitate this. Surveyors were put on every bus and interviewed one person from each party of travellers. Due to the amount of information being sought, some of the questions were on a supplementary postage paid form for self completion by the interviewee.

The survey revealed that some 539 and 526 parties used the service on Wednesday and Saturday respectively. The response rate for those participating in the interview survey *and* returning the questionnaire was 66 per cent on the Wednesday and 47 per cent on the Saturday.

Photograph 9.3 Route around the Inner Circuit Road

Photograph 9.4 Bus lane on the inbound A4 section

Journey Purpose As expected there was a considerable difference between Wednesday and Saturday. As Table 9.1 shows, on the Wednesday 70 per cent of journeys were for commuting while on Saturday this figure was only 6 per cent. On Saturdays shopping was the dominant purpose accounting for 82 per cent of all parties, contrasting with 18 per cent on Wednesdays.

User Origins For both the Wednesday and Saturday surveys user origins were similar. Around one third came from the A4 corridor outside Bristol; Keynsham, Saltford and Bath, with a similar proportion from south and east Bristol. The remainder largely came from the area outside Bristol in an arc from the eastern Mendips, Midsomer Norton/Radstock through Frome to the west Wiltshire towns. Table 9.2 provides further details.

Table 9.1
Journey purpose

Journey Purpose	Wednesday	Saturday
	% of parties	% of parties
Commuting	70.3	6.2
Shopping	18.2	81.9
Employer's business	3.0	0.5
Other	8.5	11.4

Alternative Modes Table 9.3 provides details of the transport modes that respondents said they would have used if the park and ride had not been available. Here again there are substantial differences between the Wednesday and Saturday responses. On Wednesday 55.5 per cent said they would have used car for the entire journey compared to 72 per cent on Saturday. On Wednesday 40 per cent said they would otherwise use public transport with just over 1 per cent who would have walked or cycled; this compares with the Saturday situation where some 16 per cent would otherwise use public transport and none would have walked or cycled. Generated travel also shows significant differences with 3.3 per cent on Wednesday, compared to 12.2 per cent on Saturday, saying they would either have travelled elsewhere or wouldn't have made a journey at all. Some 6.5 per cent of respondents on Wednesdays and 2 per cent on Saturdays said that, if the scheme had not been available, they would have sometimes used the car and sometimes public transport. It was therefore assumed that these respondents would have equally divided their journeys between car and public transport.

Table 9.2
User origins

User Origin	Wednesday	Saturday
	% of parties	% of parties
Bath/Saltford/ Keynsham	33.4	34.1
South & East Bristol	34.4	27.4
South East Avon	12.6	11.8
Rest of Avon	7.5	13.1
West Wiltshire	5.8	6.6
East Somerset	5.1	5.6
Other	1.2	1.4

Calculation of the changes in the distance travelled by car The data was analysed in three sets, the first being those who said they would have used the car, the second being those who said they would have travelled by car on some occasions and by public transport on others, the third being those who would have travelled by public transport/other non car mode/would not have travelled at all.

For each party the change in the distance travelled by car was calculated, within the Bristol conurbation, outside Bristol, within all urban areas, within rural areas and overall. These were then aggregated and factored up to arrive at total figures for all users of the scheme, it being assumed that the Wednesday results are representative of other weekdays and can therefore be multiplied by five. In calculating the changes, assumptions had to be made about the routes that would have been taken. It being assumed that M or A class roads would have been used except where the origin or destination did not lie on one and/or where the use of such a road would have resulted in a significantly longer route. The results for Mondays to Fridays and for Saturdays are set out in Tables 9.4 and 9.5.

Changes in Monday to Friday Car Usage In respect of those parties that would have otherwise travelled by car all the way to the city centre the estimated reduction in car usage is almost 12,000kms per week. Within the Bristol built up area the saving was actually just over 15,000kms but this was offset by just over an additional 3,000kms travelled outside Bristol. This additional distance was a result of some users cutting across from other radial routes, such as the A37, to reach the park and ride site.

Considering those who said they would sometimes use car and sometimes other modes, there would appear to be a small overall increase in car usage. The saving of some 800kms within Bristol being more than offset by an increase of 1,600kms outside the city. This is a result of the distance from the park and ride site to the city centre being less than the average distance from the journey origins to the site.

Table 9.3
Alternative modes

Alternative Mode	Wednesday % of parties	Saturday % of parties
Car/Van	55.5	72.1
Motorcycle	0.0	0.0
Bus/Coach	28.1	15.0
Taxi	0.0	0.0
Train	11.9	0.8
Cycle	0.7	0.0
Walk	0.6	0.0
Travel Elsewhere	1.3	7.7
Wouldn't make journey	2.0	4.5

For those who would otherwise have used a non car mode, principally bus or train, there is an estimated increase of over 14,000 vehicle kms per week. Within Bristol, an increase of some 1,500kms results from people who would otherwise have used the bus, driving to the site from parts of the south and east of the city. Not surprisingly outside Bristol there is a considerable increase of almost 13,000kms.

Setting the savings produced by some users against the increases of others produces an estimated *increase* in overall car usage of just over 3,000kms per week. This incorporates a reduction within Bristol of some 14,500 kms but an increase outside of over 17,500. Considering all urban areas the reduction is just over 11,000kms as the reduction in Bristol is offset by an increase of some 3,000kms in other towns and cities such as Keynsham and Bath.

Changes in Saturday car usage Due to the much smaller proportion of parties who said they would otherwise have used public transport, the picture on Saturdays is significantly different. Whilst, as for Monday to Friday, those who would otherwise have travelled by car produced a reduction in car usage and those who would have used other modes for some or all of their journey produced an increase, the overall picture is one of an estimated *decrease* in the distance travelled by car of just over 1,000kms. A decrease in Bristol of over 3,500kms being only partially offset by an increase of some 2,500kms outside. Again considering all urban areas there is a reduction in some 3,100kms, the reduction in Bristol being offset to a small extent by an additional 500kms in other urban areas.

Table 9.4
Changes in distance travelled by car, Mon - Fri (kms/week)

	Car Users	Car/Public Transport	Non car mode	All Users
Within Bristol	-15,138	-782	+1,481	- 14,439
Outside Bristol	+3,290	+1,632	+12,729	+17,651
Within Urban Areas	-14,040	-517	+3,318	- 11,239
In Non Bristol	+1,098	+265	+1,836	+3,199
Rural Areas	+2,192	+1,368	+10,893	+14,453
Overall	-11,848	+850	+14,210	+3,212

Changes in car usage over a full week Table 9.6 sets out the changes in Monday to Friday and Saturday car usage and the overall change for the six day week the service operates.

This shows that as a result of the park and ride scheme there is an estimated *increase* in car usage of 2,000kms per week. Within Bristol there is a reduction of 17,600kms but this is more than offset by an increase elsewhere of 19,600kms. For urban areas outside Bristol there is an increase of 3,600kms producing a net reduction of 14,000kms in all urban areas. Within rural areas the increase in car usage is of the order of 16,000kms.

Overall change in motor vehicle usage To determine the overall impact of the service on vehicle usage it is also necessary to consider the distance travelled by the buses operating the service. The service operates 349 return journeys on Monday to Friday and 55 return journeys on a Saturday, making a total of 404 per week. The distance travelled by the buses, including off service to/from the depot, is 4833kms on Monday to Friday and 956kms on Saturday, a total of 5,789Kms per week. Table 9.7 includes the changes in the distances travelled by car and bus to arrive at figures for the overall change in motor vehicle usage.

151

Table 9.5
Changes in distance travelled by car, Saturdays (kms)

	Car Users	Car/Public Transport Users	Non car mode Users	All Users
Within Bristol	-3,839	-34	+243	-3,630
Outside Bristol	+561	+60	+1,916	+2,537
Within Urban Areas	-3,677	-25	+568	-3,134
In Non Bristol Urban Areas	+162	+9	+325	+496
Rural Areas	+399	+51	+1,591	+2,041
Overall	-3,278	+26	+2,159	-1,093

Table 9.6
Changes in distance travelled by by car (kms)

	Mon - Fri	Saturday	All Week
Within Bristol	-14,439	-3,630	-18,069
Outside Bristol	+17,651	+2,537	+20,188
Within Urban Areas	-11,239	-3,134	-14,373
In Non Bristol Urban Areas	+3,199	+496	+3,695
Rural Areas	+14,453	+2,041	+16,494
Overall	+3,212	-1,093	+2,119

The result of including the bus operation is to increase the additional distance attributable to the scheme on Mondays to Fridays by a factor of 2.5, and to almost wipe out the reduction in vehicle usage achieved on Saturdays. Of course the environmental impact of a bus and a car are not the same. The conventional assumption (as used by Papoulias and Heggie 1976) is that the impact of a bus is three times that of a car. On such an assumption the negative impact of the

Table 9.7
Overall changes in distance travelled by motor vehicle
(car & bus) (kms)

	Mon - Fri	Saturday	All Week
Within Bristol	-9,606	-2,674	-12,280
Outside Bristol	+17,651	+2,537	+20,188
Within Urban Areas	-6,406	-2,178	-8,584
In Non Bristol Urban Areas	+3,199	+496	+3,695
Rural Areas	+14,453	+2,041	+16,494
Overall	+8,045	-137	+7,908

Monday to Friday service would be significantly increased and the impact of the Saturday service would change from marginally positive to negative. Indeed the benefits to the Bristol urban area would also be wiped out on Mondays to Fridays although they would remain positive on Saturdays. The impact on all urban areas would change from positive to negative. Table 9.8 illustrates the effect of such an assumption.

Table 9.8
Overall changes in distance travelled by motor vehicle

Distance travelled by car and bus, weighting bus kms at x3 car kms

	Mon - Fri	Saturday	All Week
Within Bristol	+60	-762	-702
Outside Bristol	+17,651	+2,537	+20,188
Within Urban Areas	+3,260	-266	+2,994
In Non Bristol Urban Areas	+3,199	+496	+3,695
Rural Areas	+14,453	+2,041	+16,494
Overall	+17,711	+1,775	+19,486

153

However, the environmental impact of motor vehicle use is greater within urban areas than rural areas. Fuel consumption will normally be greater due to the more congested conditions with the result that exhaust emissions will be higher for a given distance travelled. Furthermore, as population densities are higher, a greater number of people will experience the reduced air quality, noise and visual intrusion. Consequently it could be argued that savings in urban car usage should be valued at a higher rate than savings in rural areas. An estimate was made of the change in fuel consumption likely to be produced by the scheme. As details relating to the fuel consumption of the cars parked at the site are not known assumptions have to be made. Assuming an average consumption of 14.30lts/100kms (20mpg) in urban areas and 7.15lts/100kms (40mpg) in rural areas, the saving in fuel consumed in urban areas would be 2,053 litres and the additional consumed in rural areas would be 1,178, litres a net saving of 875 litres. However, the fuel consumed by the buses must also be taken into account and this was obtained from the bus company. At an average of 41.66lts/100kms (6.86mpg) this produced a weekly consumption of 2,412 litres. At these figures the overall impact is an increase in fuel consumed of 1,537 litres per week. On top of this an allowance would need to be made for the fuel consumed in the operation of the site, primarily electricity for the lighting.

Summary

At the time it was surveyed, the Bristol park and ride scheme would appear to be producing a net increase in car usage and fuel consumed and therefore a decline in the environmental sustainability of the transport system. Whilst the survey suggests that there is a reduction in car usage on Saturdays this would seem to be more than outweighed by an increase on Mondays to Fridays. Within Bristol there appears to be a significant saving in car kilometres but this has to be set against the larger increase outside. When the impact of the bus service is also taken into account even the benefits within Bristol are largely negated. These findings are consistent with those of the 1975 TSU survey undertaken following the opening of the Oxford scheme (Papoulias and Heggie 1976).

Change in patronage since the survey

Since the survey was undertaken, use of the Bristol service has continued to grow. By the middle of March 1995 the number of parties had increased by 37 per cent on Wednesdays and 37.5 per cent on Saturdays. If the alternative modes of these additional parties, together with the distribution of their origins, are in the same proportion as those surveyed in March 1994 then this would produce a decline in the overall environmental impact of the service on Mondays to Fridays but an improvement on Saturdays. However, in that the service is still being operated by the same number of buses, it should now be producing an environmental improvement in the Bristol urban area even when taking into account their operation. This is illustrated in Table 9.9.

Table 9.9
Overall changes in distance travelled by motor vehicle

Distance travelled by car and bus, weighting bus kms at x3 car kms based on March 1995 patronage levels

	Mon - Fri	Saturday	All Week
Within Bristol	-5,282	-2,123	-7,405
Outside Bristol	+24,182	+3,488	+27,670
Within Urban Areas	-898	-1,441	-2,339
In Non Bristol Urban Areas	+4,382	+682	+5,064
Rural Areas	+19,801	+2,806	+22,607
Overall	+18,900	+1,365	+20,265

Can the service produce an environmental gain?

On Mondays to Fridays the net environmental loss is a result of the high abstraction from public transport together with the fact that outside the peaks, the numbers carried on many of the journeys is low. Whilst reducing the off-peak service frequency would reduce the environmental impact of the bus operation it could deter those users who value the flexibility offered by a frequent service even if they don't often take advantage of it. Simply attracting more users, given a 40 per cent take from public transport and the same distribution of journey origins, actually makes the overall situation worse although it does produce a net benefit within Bristol. To reduce and overturn the environmental deficit it is therefore necessary to attract more users who would otherwise travel by car and return others to bus and rail. To attract more car users it is probably necessary to strengthen traffic restraint measures such as tighter parking controls in the city centre and the imposition of economic and/or regulatory measures to deter driving in the city. To return others to bus and rail it will be necessary to improve the quality of the service they offer and/or change the cost of using them compared to the park and ride.

The implementation of improvements to other public transport services and of traffic restraint measures is included in the Transport Plan. However, the restraint measures are proposed in the longer term and are likely to be rather more politically controversial than improving public transport. This is particularly so in the context of the planned 1997 opening of the Cribbs Causeway regional shopping complex, a major competitor to the Bristol city centre shopping area in the form of a regional shopping complex with 7,000 parking places adjacent to M5 Junction 17. The opening of the planned sites on other radials would reduce the considerable diversions some users make to reach the site and could also produce some improvement to the performance of this scheme. However, if similar abstraction rates occur at these sites then the overall problem could be compounded.

On Saturdays the much lower abstraction rate from public transport does result in a net reduction in car usage but, taking into account the operation of the bus service, the overall impact at the time of the survey was approximately neutral. Here, unlike the Mondays to Fridays situation, the subsequent increase in usage would appear to have improved the environmental performance of the scheme.

General conclusion

The Bristol study provides further confirmation that, in environmental terms, the success of park and ride cannot simply be equated with patronage. Some of the earlier studies identified a substantial number of users who, in the absence of the scheme, would have used informal park and ride, or public transport for their whole journey, or may not have made the journey at all. This is also the case in Bristol. Such circumstances produce a situation where, at least in the case of the Bristol scheme, bus park and ride would presently appear to have a negative environmental impact. Whether this is the case in other towns and cities will depend on a number of factors including the distances users travel to the park and ride site(s) and the characteristics of the bus service.

The Bristol study also suggests that, if a level of abstraction from public transport sufficient to undermine the environmental benefits of the scheme is to be avoided, the provision of park and ride on corridors presently with extensive public transport services should not be pursued. However, it is probable that these are the very corridors which have sufficient demand to support the provision of a service. Consequently if abstraction is to be minimised careful attention must be paid to the relative price and quality of the services. Schemes also need to be accompanied by measures to restrain the use of the car within the urban area served. Nevertheless, one is left with the perception that, except on those corridors where public transport would be very costly to provide, it would be preferable on both environmental and social grounds if travellers to the city centre could be persuaded to leave their cars at home and make the whole journey by public transport. Not only would this conserve resources and reduce pollution but the additional demand and level of services provided would benefit all travellers, not just those with access to a car.

Note

1   The views expressed in this chapter are those of the author and do not necessarily coincide with those of Avon County Council or its successor authorities.

References

Association of District Councils (1992), *Survey of Park and Ride Schemes December 1991*, Association of District Councils: London.

Bixby, R. W. (1991), *Bus Park and Ride in the UK,* School of Planning Oxford Polytechnic, March 1991.

Centro (1992), 'Coventry Park and Ride Survey' Part 2, (Ref No B53.92). Centro: Birmingham.

County of Avon (1990), *Park and Ride For Bristol:- Development of Bus Based Schemes Preliminary Report*, Department of Highways, Transport and Engineering: Bristol.

County of Avon (1993), *Transport Plan 1993-2013 Consultation Document*, Department of Highways, Transport and Engineering, February 1993, County of Avon: Bristol.

County of Avon (1994), *Implementation of Bus Priorities in Bristol*, Report to Low Energy Consultative Committee 29th April 1994.

Day, C. (1992), 'Traffic Congestion and the Survival of an Historic City', *Town and Country Planning Summer School Proceedings, The Planner*, 27th November, Vol 78, No.21, pp.52-54.

Department of Engineering and Recreation (1991), *Park and Ride in Oxford*, Oxford City Council: Oxford.

English Historic Towns Forum (1993), *Bus-Based Park and Ride: A Good Practice Guide*, Avon County Council for EHFT: Bristol.

Jones, P. (1989), 'Oxford - An Evolving Transport Policy', *Built Environment* Vol. 15 Nos 3/4, pp. 231-243.

MVA Consultancy (1991), *BRITES - Bristol Integrated Transport and Environmental Study, Final Report*, November 1991. MVA: Woking.

Newson, N. (1994), 'Town Centre Traffic Management; The Key Role of Park and Ride'. *Town Centre Traffic Management Seminar*, PTRC: London.

Papoulias, D.B. and Heggie I.G. (1976), 'A comparative evaluation of forecast and use of park-and-ride in Oxford', *Traffic Engineering and Control* Vol. 13, pp. 144-149.

Parkhurst, G. (1994), 'Park and Ride: Could it lead to an increase in car traffic?' Paper presented to the *22nd PTRC European Transport Forum* 12 - 16 September 1994 University of Warwick, PTRC: London.

Pullen, W.T. and Silcock D.T. (1991), 'The Impact of Park and Ride on City Centre Congestion: A case study of the Tyne and Wear Metro', *19th PTRC European Transport Forum, Public Transport Planning and Operations* University of Sussex, PTRC: London.

Richardson, T. (1994), 'The Norwich Experience', Paper to Aston University Conference: *Park and Ride: Increasing the chances of success*, 20th April 1994.

Rigby, J. and Jones D. (1991), 'Environmental Transport Policies: Putting the theory into practice in York', *Traffic Engineering and Control*, Vol. 32, pp. 516-521.

Rivers, S. and Casement, R. (1992), 'Keeping the Traffic at Bay', *The Surveyor*, 12 November 1992, pp. 18-19.

Shropshire County Council (1994), 1994/95 *Transport Policies and Programme* Appendix 2 Integrated Transport Plan for Shrewsbury (Package Proposals).

10 Coordinating facility provision and new housing development: impacts on car and local facility use

John Winter and Stuart Farthing

The focus of this chapter is the examination of facility provision on major housing schemes, and how local environmental policy can help promote sustainable travel patterns; the discussion is based on the results of a major research project[1].

We will begin with a brief discussion of the background to the research project, dealing with government policy guidance and relevant academic research, and identifying the key research objectives to be dealt with in this paper. This will be followed by an introduction to the case study developments in Avon with which we have been concerned. Next the research methods used during the project will be covered, followed by a discussion of the main substantive issues raised and explored by the research, and we conclude with a discussion of our findings, with reference in particular to the preparation of relevant environmental policy.

Government policy and the academic context of the research

The academic and policy context to our project has a variety of different strands. Most directly has been the commitment over the past 10 years of a research team at UWE to the examination of the quality of the environments being created on new large scale, private sector housing developments, an area which has been given little direct attention by other researchers, despite the continued scale of housing provision in this form. We have looked at various dimensions of these new developments over time, such as, the development process involved in the creation of large scale schemes, and consumer reaction to such developments, both areas that had previously been largely neglected (see Farthing and Winter 1988; Coombes, Farthing and Winter 1990; Winter, Coombes and Farthing 1993). The consumers or residents of these developments are rarely, if at all, consulted in relation to the creation of the environment, despite the fact that they are making the most significant purchase in their lives, in setting up mortgages and buying homes.

A second and perhaps most significant strand is the publication of PPG13 (DoE 1994) marking a sea-change in government guidance, advocating sustainable development in general and underlining the importance of accessibility to local facilities in particular. This PPG, in line with the European Commission's Green Paper on the Urban Environment (CEG 1990), and supported by such writers as Elkin, McLaren and Hillman (1991) and Sherlock (1991), views the compact city as the sustainable city, and sees the peripheral housing estates typical of the 1970s and 1980s as highly inefficient particularly in terms of travel patterns. We consider such outright condemnation of peripheral estates premature and the research reported here aims to assess the performance of these developments in relation to local facility provision.

An important strand in the policy context is the renewed interest in PPG13 (DoE 1994) in the integration of provision for housing and local facilities. Neighbourhood planning as planning orthodoxy had fallen from official grace by the 1970s, for a variety of economic and ideological reasons, though in our experience local authorities have in practice, continued to plan for neighbourhoods in large scale residential developments through local plans, development briefs and design control albeit usually in a partial rather than in the comprehensive form found in new towns in the 1950s and 1960s. A key dimension to neighbourhood planning is the determination of the facilities to be provided. PPG13 refers to 'everyday activities' as if there is agreement on what these should be, and does indeed produce a list identifying shopping, play areas, open space, schools, health centres, branch libraries and local offices of the local authority. But Hillman and his co-workers have produced different lists (Hillman, Henderson and Whalley 1973; Hillman, Henderson and Whalley 1976; Hillman and Whalley 1983), and there is little empirical work to establish the frequency of local use or indeed those visited on an 'everyday basis'. It was therefore part of the object of this project to chart both the nature and range of such provision and to help operationalise the concept of 'everyday activities'.

PPG13 makes some quite strong statements about the relationship between local provision and the increased use of cycling and walking, which is supported in part by the work of Hillman, Henderson and Whalley (1976) which found that the more local the facility the more likely that people will walk to it. But research to date on trips to facilities has focused on car travel and neglected more sustainable modes, an omission reinforced by the National Travel statistics and surveys, which also ignores trips of under 1 mile; another limitation of such research from our point of view is that the work has concentrated on urban areas where high density often presents wider options for local travel, than typically found on peripheral estates.

An important dimension to a fuller understanding of travel patterns is the examination of the socio-economic and other key factors that affect choice. Research has shown that there are a multitude of factors - gender, age, density of development, distance to facilities, car availability, unemployment and children in the household - that impact on travel behaviour; relationships have, unsurprisingly, been shown to be highly complex, and the difficulty of interpreting findings further complicated by a focus on the household as a whole, rather than the individual, when it is our view that trip behaviour may vary greatly for example, between men and women, adult and child, within the group (Guy and Wrigley, 1987, Pas 1984, Hanson and Schwab 1987). Our current work is therefore based on the analysis of the travel patterns of individuals.

Research objectives

1. To identify the level and range of local facility provision on major peripheral private sector housing estates.

2. To identify the extent to which local provision of facilities leads to local use.

3. To examine the impact of local provision on the length of journeys to facilities.

4. To examine the extent to which local provision leads to the use of environmentally friendly modes of transport and discourages the use of the car.

5. To examine the extent to which local provision reduces the length of trips by car.

6. To identify the main socio-economic and other key factors that affect the individual's trip behaviour.

Case study developments in Avon

Figure 10.1 illustrates the geographical location of the 5 case study sites in Avon that we have been dealing with. They are 5 of the principal areas of new private sector residential development within the county, and vary in scale and timescale of development as shown in Table 10.1. All are considered as major developments, that is over 500 dwellings, but they vary in terms of their location to existing built up areas (see Figure 10.1); Bradley Stoke North and South and Worle are large scale extensions to Bristol and Weston, while Longwell Green is infill development on the periphery of the Bristol/Kingswood urban area, and Peasedown St John a major village expansion some miles from Bath.

All the case study sites have substantial development in place on the ground: Longwell Green and North Worle are both substantially complete now and have been under construction for the longest period. The other sites are well underway in terms of construction.

161

Table 10.1

Scale of developments

	Dwellings	Timescale
Bradley Stoke (North & South)	8,500	1987 - 2000
Longwell Green	2,500	1979 - 1996
Peasedown St John	1,000	1989 - date
North Worle	4,500	1975 - date

Research methods

The research was based on two surveys. The physical survey of local facility provision on the ground took place in the period January - March 1994. Our data on the use of local facilities was by means of a postal questionnaire which we sent to a random sample of addresses in each of the developments. The facilities included in our inquiry are based on the range of facilities that planning authorities are typically looking to provide on new developments, and supplemented by others suggested by Hillman, Henderson and Whalley (1976). Recent research for the DoE/DoT (1993) had talked about the use of local centres which we felt to be an ambiguous concept, and therefore did not use.

We asked about the last trip that the person who was to complete the questionnaire, had made to a particular facility. We settled on this as a way forward after some debate. Initial consideration was given to a number of different methods of understanding residents' trip patterns, all with their own particular set of problems. We could have asked people where they 'typically' went shopping, for example, but we decided to ask for the last time they had visited a particular facility so we would be looking at actual behaviour rather than impressionistic information.

We wanted information about the use of facilities by all residents (including children of 5 or over) but we felt that it was unrealistic to ask all members of a household to complete the questionnaire. The solution we arrived at was that the person who should complete the questionnaire was the person whose birthday was closest to the date on which they received the questionnaire through the post. The idea was that we should end up with a more or less random sample of the population living in these areas.

The questionnaire generated 624 responses, detailing 4,600 trips, evenly distributed across the 5 case study developments. This constitutes a 25% response rate which though typical of postal questionnaires, is not high enough to provide full confidence in the 'representativeness' of our data.

From our analysis of 1991 census data we know that all our case study sites have a similar population structure, typical of owner occupied housing developments,

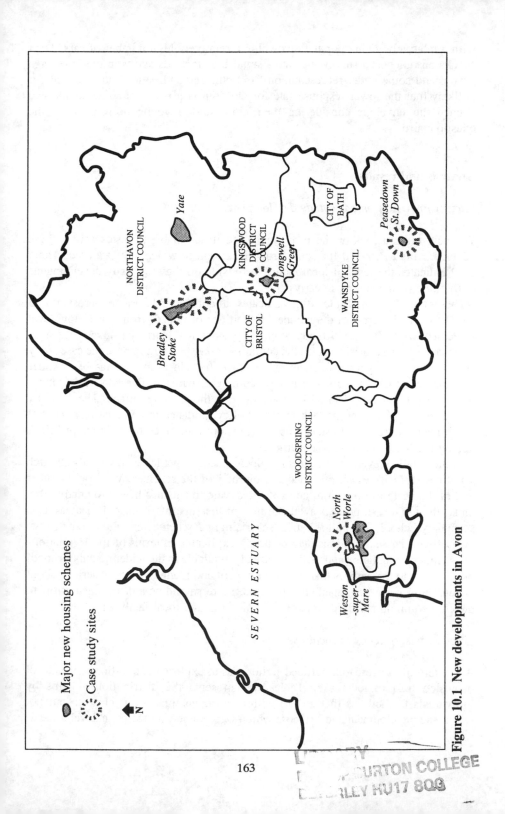

Figure 10.1 New developments in Avon

LIBRARY
BURTON COLLEGE
BEVERLEY HU17 8QG

with a relatively young population owning a relatively high number of cars. Data checks on our postal survey indicate a small bias towards adults in the 25-34 age groups and some under-representation from children and young adults (16-24); it is likely that the lower response rate for children is a result of some adults who opened the envelope considering their children too young to respond to the questionnaire.

Analysis and results

Facility provision on case study developments

We now turn to look at the provision of facilities in broad terms across these developments as context for considering the extent to which they are used. Table 10.2 indicates the level of local facility provision on the case study developments at the time of the survey in early 1994.

The totals line in Table 10.2 indicates a considerable range across the 5 developments in terms of the number of facilities provided, from a very low level in Peasedown St John to virtually complete provision at North Worle. At first sight this may appear surprising given the common population structure of the case study sites. But it is largely explicable by the fact that North Worle has been under development for 20 years and is now complete, while in Peasedown St John a number of the missing facilities are available in the existing village. The disparity may also in part reflect the lack of clear policy guidance in this area from central government, in relation to standards of provision, reinforced by different priorities among the local authorities concerned.

At the detailed level, only 1 amenity, open space, is available universally, though 10 of the 19 facilities are provided in 4 out of 5 of the schemes. While at the other end of the scale of provision, none of the developments has been provided with a bank, though a cash point is available in 1 of the supermarkets, only 1 area has a secondary school, and perhaps most surprisingly 2 schemes are without their own post office. These variations may be partly explicable in terms of local variations in catchment population and facilities already available in the wider neighbourhood, but it seems to the authors that if as government and planners, we are serious about encouraging more sustainable trip patterns, there should be a determined effort to develop common standards for the provision of such local facilities.

Local provision leads to local use

A key aim of our research outlined earlier was to explore the question : Does local provision lead to local use? Table 10.3 presents the distribution of trips by individuals to facilities that are i) within the development, ii) close to but not within the development and iii) those which were some way from the development.

Table 10.2
Provision of facilities on each development

Facility/Development	Bradley Stoke North	Bradley Stoke South	Longwell Green	Peasedown St John	North Worle	Total Number
Shopping:						
Bank	N	N	N	N	N	0
Chemist	Y	Y	Y	N	Y	4
Food shop	Y	Y	Y	N	Y	4
Newsagent	Y	Y	Y	N	Y	4
Post Office	Y	N	Y	N	Y	3
Supermarket	Y	Y	Y	N	Y	4
Recreation:						
Leisure/sports facility	Y	Y	N	N	Y	3
Open space	Y	Y	Y	Y	Y	5
Play area	Y	Y	Y	N	Y	4

Table 10.2 (continued)
Provision of facilities on each development

Facility/Development	Bradley Stoke North	Bradley Stoke South	Longwell Green	Peasedown St John	North Worle	Total Number
Education:						
College	N	N	N	N	N	0
Secondary school	N	N	N	N	N	1
Primary school	Y	N	Y	N	Y	3
Health:						
Dentist	N	N	Y	Y	Y	3
Doctor	Y	N	Y	Y	Y	4
Health centre	Y	N	Y	Y	Y	4
Community:						
Community centre	Y	Y	Y	N	Y	4
Church	Y	Y	N	N	Y	3
Library	N	Y	Y	Y	Y	4
Public house	Y	Y	Y	N	Y	4
Total number	14	11	14	5	17	

166

Table 10.3

Distribution of trips by geographical relationship to the development ranked by % of trips made within the development

	Super market	Secondary school	Newsagent	. .	Post Office	Health centre	Doctor	Foodshop	Chemist
				. .					
				. .					
Within the development	76	68	67	. .	60	59	57	55	50
Close to the development	21	23	23	. .	31	35	31	31	35
Away from the development	3	9	9	. .	7	5	12	14	14

Table 10.3 (continued)

Distribution of trips by geographical relationship to the development ranked by % of trips made within the development

	Primary school	Play area	Community centre	Public house	Open space		Church	Library	Dentist	Leisure facility
Within the development	47	44	42	41	35	.	21	15	12	7
Close to the development	47	37	53	34	24	.	47	57	61	36
Away from the development	7	19	4	25	39	.	32	29	27	55

The data includes trips only where the facility concerned is available within the development, and the results are ranked according to the percentage of trips made to those facilities provided within the development.

The general message is that provision of local facilities within the development seems to have a varied impact on the destination of trips. It is useful at this point to distinguish 4 different groupings within the results, as presented in Table 10.3. The first group including supermarkets, secondary schools and newsagents, shows the facilities where provision at the local level has had a very marked effect on trip behaviour with more than two thirds of trips being made to facilities within the development. For these facilities then, local provision leads to local use on a massive scale. The second group of five facilities (post office, health centre, doctor, food shop and chemist) attracts 50% or more of trips to facilities within the development, highlighting further the positive impact of local provision; it will be noted that top of this group are post offices, which are provided within only 2 of the 5 case study developments.

The third group of five facilities (primary school, play area, community centre, public house and open space) still shows considerable demand for local facilities with a third or more of all trips to these facilities being carried out within the development; so where there is local provision within this group it can have a significant impact on travel patterns, though clearly it will not satisfy all needs, and people are likely also to travel outside of the development attracted to better quality, or different facilities elsewhere. In the case of primary schools, perhaps, the limited capacity of provision on new developments may require children to travel to surrounding schools, whatever their parents might want.

The final grouping of facilities at the bottom end of the spectrum (church, dentist, library, leisure facility) illustrate areas where local provision has much less impact on local use and travel behaviour, generally because these facilities tend to be more varied and specialist in nature. For example visits to the dentist are relatively infrequent, normally, and because of its highly specialist nature, people are likely to be highly discriminating about their choice of practice, which may lead them to stay with their previous practice even where this is at a distance. Churches and leisure facilities encompass a wide variety of specialist tastes which local provision cannot aspire to cover, and often involve membership of communities which develop strong loyalties and will survive a move to a distant address.

These results indicate then, that local provision may produce highly significant levels of local use, for a wide range, but not for all facilities often provided, indicating significant potential for sustainable benefits, provided policy is well informed and discriminating.

Local provision cuts journey length

The policy guidance suggests that the provision of local facilities is the key to reducing journey lengths. Does the provision of a local facility reduce the length of journeys that people make? We need to compare the situations where the residents have a local opportunity for using a particular facility and situations where residents do not have that opportunity. What impact does the lack of a local opportunity have on the distance travelled?

In order to reduce this analysis to manageable proportions and to operationalise the concept of facilities used as part of everyday activities, we have identified a smaller group of facilities which we call the 'day to day eight'. They have been selected on the basis that they score highest across three criteria i) the number of developments on which they are provided, ii) the level of local use and, iii) the frequency of trips. In practice the last two are highly correlated. The 'everyday eight' are: foodshop, newsagent, open space, post office, primary school, pub, supermarket, and secondary school.

Regression analysis was undertaken with the straight-line distance from home to the facility as the dependent variable and a range of independent dummy variables (age, gender, employment status, presence of children in the household, car-ownership). The results are shown in Table 10.4 for home-based trips. In this table we distinguish between the importance of local provision (which is the crucial policy variable in this analysis) and other factors which may have an impact on the situation but which are much less amenable to policy influence. Only variables that are statistically significant are shown in the table and they are indicated by abbreviated variable names. A plus in front of the variable in Table 10.4 indicates that the category of variable in question tends to increase journey length compared with the 'suppressed' category whilst a minus sign indicates that the category of the variable in question tends to reduce journey length. They reveal that for 7 of the 8 key facilities we have identified the impact of local provision is to reduce average journey lengths. The only exception is open space, and here the problem is that open space of one sort or another is present on each development investigated and hence we cannot assess the impact of lack of provision through regression analysis.

Other factors play a part in the distance travelled. The presence of children in the household reduced journey lengths for trips to post offices and to primary schools. In the first case it is probably due to payment of child benefit at local post offices and in the latter case it is likely that educational trips by children to primary schools are locally orientated but that trips to schools by adults for other leisure purposes may be to more distant schools.

Car ownership not surprisingly has an extensive and complex impact on journey lengths. The sign of the variable in our regressions is generally negative for households with one car, suggesting that they tend to travel less far than those with two or more cars; the sign for those with no cars, however, is positive which indicates that non-car-owning households when they make trips to supermarkets and primary schools are longer than those made by households with two or more cars; the explanation here is probably that they are dependent on local bus transport and that these routes tend not to give such good access to the local facilities. However for food shops, the sign for non-car-owning households is negative indicating that they tend to use local opportunities more than those with two or more cars; the explanation here is probably that these trips are made by foot.

Table 10.4

The influence of local provision and other factors on distance travelled

Facility	Distance travelled	
	Influence of local provision	Influence of other factors
Supermarket	-LOCSUP**	+CARO**
Foodshop	-LOCFOOD**	-CARO**
Newsagent	-LOCNEWS**	
Post office	-LOCPOST**	-CAR1* -CHILDREN**
Open space	na	+AGE2** +MALE*
Primary school	-LOCPRIM*	-CHILDREN* +CARO** -CAR1*
Secondary school	-LOCSEC*	
Public house	-LOCPUB**	

*= 95% significance level
**= 99% significance level

This analysis offers, then, further encouragement to planners to provide a range of local provision, with confirmation that such provision leads to shorter average journeys. It confirms also that the presence of children and car ownership levels have an impact on journey lengths, factors which should be taken carefully into account when planning such developments.

At this point we turn to consider the extent to which more sustainable modes are used for trips to local facilities. The first highly disappointing fact to note is that despite relatively high levels of bicycle ownership the level of use (2% of trips) is so low that the data cannot be productively analysed. Our discussion in this section concentrates therefore on walking trips.

There are two stages to our analysis. We consider first the impact of facility provision alone on walking trips; does local provision encourage walking trips, as suggested by the analysis in PPG13 and does this lead to a significant switch in mode from car to foot? Second we consider the situation where people choose to use local facilities - to what extent do they also choose walking?

The results of the first analysis are shown in Table 10.5. The influence of local provision on mode of transport used, was analysed by means of logistic regression, which computes the likelihood of a dichotomous dependent variable (walk/not walk) given a series of independent variables. The independent variable that we are primarily interested in is the provision of a facility on the new housing development. Once again variables are only included in the table if they are statistically significant and the direction of impact is indicated by a plus or minus sign. The results indicate that local accessibility alone is not a strong influence on travel mode. Of our 8 facilities, only for trips to secondary schools and to the pub does local provision itself encourage walking trips; this reinforces the case for local provision of secondary education if sustainability is a serious policy consideration, and establishes a strong case for pubs where there are additional good reasons for leaving the car at home. Once again, the impact of provision for open space cannot be evaluated.

The regression analysis also identifies other factors which have an impact on the mode of travel to facilities. There is as expected (since non car owning households do not have the option of using the car) a strong negative impact from car ownership for a number of facilities. Persons in households with one car or two more cars were much less likely to walk than persons in non-car-owning households. This applies to trips to supermarkets, foodshops, and newsagents. Persons from households with two or more cars are less likely to walk also to the post office and to the pub. The presence of children in the household is also likely to lead to walking trips rather than other modes for supermarket, food shop, and open space trips. For open space too the 16-45 age group are less likely to walk than the over 45's.

We turn now to our second stage of analysis; whilst the provision of local facilities per se only has a significant impact in encouraging walking trips for a limited range of facilities, does the decision to use a local facility encourage people to walk? The results for home-based trips only are shown in Table 10.6. It suggests that for people in our sample, the decision to use a local rather than a more distant facility does encourage walking for 6 out of the 8 facilities, the exceptions being to the post office and to secondary school. Once again car ownership is a strong and negative influence for 5 out of the 8 facilities which suggests unsurprisingly that people in households where there is a car or cars, are less likely to choose to walk than those without.

Table 10.5

The influence of local provision and other factors
on walking to the facility

Facility	Walking to facility	
	Influence of local provision	**Influence of other factors**
Supermarket		-CAR1** -CAR2** +CHILDREN*
Foodshop		+CHILDREN** -CAR1* -CAR2* +MALE*
Newsagent		-CAR1* -CAR2*
Post office		+HOME* -CAR2*
Open space	na	+AGE2** +CHILDREN*
Primary school		
Secondary school	+LOCSEC**	
Public house	+LOCPUB**	-CAR2**

*= 95% significance level
**= 99% significance level

173

Table 10.6

The influence of local use and other factors
on walking to the facility

Facility	Walking to facility	
	Influence of local use	Influence of other factors
Supermarket	+LOCAL*	-CAR1** -CAR2** +CHILDREN*
Foodshop	+LOCAL**	+AGE2* +CHILDREN* -CAR1* -CAR2** +MALE*
Newsagent	+LOCAL*	-CAR1* -CAR2**
Post office		-CAR2**
Open space	+LOCAL**	-AGE2*
Primary school	+LOCAL*	+FULLTIME*
Secondary school		
Public house	+LOCAL**	-CAR2**

* = 95% significance level
** = 99% significance level

Thus in summary, while the provision of local facilities will itself lead to significant levels of local use, provision alone may not be enough to tempt people from their cars to walk or cycle - other incentives, for example of an environmental kind may be necessary.

The final objective of policy considered here is reducing the lengths of motorised travel. Regression analysis was used to measure the impact of local provision of facilities on trip lengths by car, controlling for the same range of personal, household and car ownership variables that we have considered before. For 5 out of the 7 facilities for which the influence of local provision can be measured (excluding once again open space), local facility provision reduces the length of car-based trips (Table 10.7). It does not influence the length of car-based trips to either primary or secondary school; the explanation here presumably being that a substantial number of these trips are by foot in any case.

Table 10.7
The influence of local provision and other factors
on length of trip by car to the facility

Facility	Length of trip by car to facility	
	Influence of local provision	Influence of other factors
Supermarket	-LOCSUP**	
Foodshop	-LOCFOOD**	-FULLTIME*
Newsagent	+LOCNEWS**	
Post office	-LOCPOST**	-CAR1* -CHILDREN*
Open space	NA	-FULLTIME** -PARTTIME* +MALE*
Primary school		-CHILDREN*
Secondary school		
Public house	+LOCPUB*	

* = 95% significance level
** = 99% significance level

175

Other factors also play a part in reducing journey lengths, controlling for local provision. Households with one car travel less far than those with two or more for trips to the post office. People in households with children travel less far to the post office and also to primary school. The reasons are likely to be similar to those given above when all trips were considered. For open space visits, employment status seems to play a part in local use. Full-time and part-time workers are more likely to use closer facilities than the groups who are economically inactive, in full-time education or unemployed. Males seem to use more distant facilities than females.

The simple positive conclusion of this part of the analysis is therefore that facility provision locally, stands out as a variable which does in general reduce journey lengths by car.

Conclusions

It is clear to us that the results of this project indicate that there is a significant sustainability dividend to be won in relation to peoples' travel patterns on major peripheral housing developments, provided there is a co-ordinated approach to the design and development of these areas at central as well as at local level.

In PPG 13 the DOE has shifted its general policy guidance framework significantly in favour of more sustainable land use patterns, but this policy shift has left new peripheral developments somewhat in limbo, with the document coming out against such developments for less than 10,000 dwellings and in favour of concentrating provision within existing urban areas. It is our view that this guidance is dangerously simplistic; first because infill and redevelopment cannotitself meet the full demand for new housing, and secondly because as the Dutch are currently finding, a commitment to the 'Compact City' can easily lead to the overcrowded city and to further loss of amenity with open space sacrificed to meet the demand for development. Government policy guidance should be reviewed to support smaller scale peripheral development as well as redevelopment and infill, in recognition that such schemes can be sustainable; the guidance should require an overall approach at local level that prioritises sustainability in terms of location, range of facilities to be provided locally and layout and design of the development, as presented below. Turning now from national to local government we distinguish the more strategic from the more local policy level.

At strategic level, regional guidance, structure plans and local plans can play an important role in ensuring that peripheral developments are more sustainable by developing policies and proposals that:

- ensure that such schemes are located on public transport routes to maximise opportunities for sustainable travel to work and major urban facilities;
- ensure schemes are located to make the best use of existing facilities;
- provide that such developments are of sufficient scale to support a wide range

of local services and facilities;

- recognise that the availability of a range of particular facilities locally can encourage energy-efficient trip behaviour, and
- reject the passivity of the 1980s and require that all major housing projects provide access to a full range of specified local facilities.

In relation to the more local level, our results indicate that local provision of facilities can lead to local use, which is itself more sustainable, but also suggest that to encourage residents to switch their behaviour further and abandon their cars in favour of walking or cycling to local amenities, will often require further incentives. Our conclusion is that this is likely to be achieved only if there is a more total approach to local policy and design of such schemes in favour of pedestrian movement and cycling. Clearly it is essential to ensure that the appropriate range of shopping and social facilities are provided locally to suit the resident population, but equally important to ensure that such trips are as convenient and attractive as possible. More specifically local plans and supplementary planning guidance should:

- ensure thorough analysis is undertaken of local facility provision and local demand in the area around the proposed development;
- project the likely household and population characteristics of the new residents over time, paying particular attention to car ownership levels and the number of children;
- identify the facilities needed, which will include normally one or more of each of the 'day-to-day eight' - foodshop, newsagent, open space, post office, primary school, pub, supermarket and secondary school; more specialised uses such as churches, dentists and leisure facilities should be provided only where need is clearly established;
- group facilities to maximise convenience and market prospects;
- ensure the most convenient location for centres to minimise average walking distances;
- give priority to the design of high amenity footpaths and cycleways within networks of high quality open spaces, providing direct access to centres;
- provide high quality environments in centres emphasising pedestrian comfort and constraining cars;
- give early attention to the planning of local public transport networks, to link the more remote housing areas;
- confirm the planning department's responsibility for the co-ordination of facility provision across the public and private sectors, and
- be positive about the potential of Section 106 Agreements to provide for local facilities.

It is our view that a co-ordinated approach to the planning and environmental design of peripheral estates, as indicated above, will not only lead to the local use of facilities on such estates, but also tempt many to leave their cars in the garage, and walk, or dust down the bicycle instead. Peripheral estates could move from being the Cinderella developments of pre-sustainable times, to models of sustainable journey patterns.

Notes

1. The research project was funded under a Polytechnics and Colleges Funding Council research programme and was conducted in association with local planning authorities in Avon.

References

Commission of the European Communities (1990), *Green paper on the Urban Environment*, COM(90), 218 CEC, Brussels.

Coombes, T., Farthing S. and Winter, J. (1991), *Environmental quality and facilities on new housing estates*, Faculty of the Built Environment WP18, UWE: Bristol.

Department of the Environment (1994), *PPG13 Transport*, HMSO: London

Department of the Environment and Department of Transport (1993), *Reducing Transport Emissions through Planning*, HMSO: London

Department of Transport (1993) *National Travel Survey 1989/91*, HMSO: London.

Elkin, T., McLaren, D. and Hillman, M. (1991), *Reviving the City - Towards Sustainable Urban Development*, Friends of the Earth: London.

Farthing, S. and Winter, J. (1988), 'Residential density and levels of satisfaction with the external residential environment' Faculty of the Built Environment WP11, UWE: Bristol.

Guy, C. and Wrigley, N. (1987), 'Walking Trips to Shops in British Cities: An empirical review and policy re-examination', *Town Planning Review*, Vol. 58, No. 1, pp. 63-79.

Hanson, S. and Schwab, M. (1987), 'Accessibility and intraurban travel', *Environment and Planning A*, Vol. 19, pp. 735-748.

Hillman, M., Henderson, I. and Whalley, A. (1973), *Personal Mobility and Transport Policy*, PEP: London.

Hillman, M., Henderson, I. and Whalley, A. (1976), *Transport Realities & Planning Policy: Studies of Friction and Freedom in Daily Travel*, PEP: London.

Hillman, M. and Whalley, A. (1983), *Energy and Personal Travel: Obstacles to Conservation*, PSI: London.

Pas, E. (1984), 'The effect of selected sociodemographic characteristics on daily travel-activity behaviour', *Environment and Planning A*, Vol. 16, pp. 571-581.

Sherlock, H. (1991) *Cities are Good for Us*, Harper Collins: London.

Winter, J., Coombes, T. and Farthing, S. (1993) 'Satisfaction with space around the home on large private sector estates: lessons from surveys in Southern England and South Wales, 1985-1989', *Town Planning Review*, Vol. 64, No. 1, pp. 65-88.

11 The sustainable use of traditional paving

Richard Guise

The floor surface of the public realm is usually the responsibility of the local authority and the state of this floorscape can provide a significant indication of the quality and effectiveness of local environmental policy. This chapter will discuss the implications of this statement and argue that a wider recognition and use of traditional paving materials is valid both in terms of delivering environmental quality and being a sustainable resource.

The proliferation of out-of-town and edge-of-town shopping centres is challenging the economic and social sustainability of town centres to such an extent that the Department of the Environment has produced guidance and research focused on the revitalisation of town centres (DoE/URBED 1994, DoE 1994). Many local authorities recognise that town centres must regain lost ground or die: they must play to their strengths - richness through diversity of activities, accessible meeting places for a variety of groups and environmental quality expressed in the townscape, the patina of age and multi-sensory stimulation of a sense of place, a local distinctiveness.

Within this context we can consider the role of floorscape of towns and town centres in particular. Criticisms of the condition and quality of floorscape is widespread. Either paving slabs are taken up and replaced with scaleless and placeless tarmacadam, or a street is pedestrianised and surfaced with the stereotype solution of redbrick paviors laid in a herringbone pattern and/or square grey concrete slabs are laid in an equally relentless pattern, which, with the addition of standard 'heritage' fingerposts bollards and waste bins are familiar in every part of Britain.

This approach has been concerning The English Historic Towns Forum and English Heritage for some time (Davies 1991). English Heritage has been so concerned that they require local authorities to fully research local paving traditions if they wish to apply for Conservation Area Partnership funds for enhancement and pedestrianisation schemes. This timely requirement should help to ensure that these

Photograph 11.1   **Traditional paving, an essential ingredient of local distinctiveness, Gold Hill, Shaftesbury**

Photograph 11.2   **The texture, colour and non verbal communication of traditional paving design, Abbey Square, Chester**

Photograph 11.3   A well conserved market town - except for the
                           pedestrian realm; the pavements

Photograph 11.4   Traditional paving scheme laid as part of an initiative
                           to revitalise the historic centre. Guimaraes, Portugal.

schemes refer to and derive from those traditions and thus solutions may reflect and contribute towards a local sense of place.

Paving that reflects local distinctiveness enhances the character of our smaller towns. We may take our town flooring materials for granted, but imagine the loss of the existing surface in the Pantiles, Tunbridge Wells, the flint cobbles of Elm Hill in Norwich, the setts of Gold Hill in Shaftesbury or the wheelers and huge cobbles in Abbey Green, Chester and the replacement of these with seamless tarmacadam (see Figures 11.1, 11.2, 11.3).

Experience has shown that investment in the quality of the public realm can change attitudes to a town centre both in terms of the 'person in the street' or of local businesses. Larger scale examples are in Birmingham and Barcelona, smaller ones in Halifax or Guimaraes in Portugal (see Figure 11.4). Retailers and householders are likely to follow this investment by improving their premises once they feel that confidence is being expressed in an area by the local authority.

Whilst in parts of some towns paving is well maintained and recognised as being part of the cherished local scene, in other districts it may be being removed and replaced with tarmacadam, whilst in other streets stretches of pavement are actually being stolen! Theft of paving and the rise of reclaimed paving material firms reflects the value and scarcity of these materials. Stretches of paving have disappeared from a number of Yorkshire towns only to reappear in paving schemes in the south of England. Similarly in Bristol quiet streets near the harbourside have also experienced the illicit removal of their pavements.

Auditing traditional paving resources

It is perhaps surprising that unlike our stock of vernacular buildings, little is known about the extent of our surviving traditional paving resource, the threats it faces, its range of materials or the lessons that can be learned in its design and layout. Local authorities whose responsibilities cover most of the public realm usually split their duties between planning and highway departments, in terms of control, design, funding, implementation and maintenance. The local authorities, possibly supported by local amenity groups are the natural focus for the recording of this stock.

It is suggested that there are three levels of recognition required:

a) Streets of acknowledged significance. Where there are substantial stretches of traditional paving in reasonable condition and with some form of protection. Conservation Area status helps to some extent, but paving cannot be 'Listed', according to recent legal opinion, as it cannot be a building, for it is laid, not erected. Indeed some earlier listed pavements have actually been withdrawn from later Schedules of Listed Buildings (e.g. Abbey Green, Chester, 1994). Even in Conservation Areas surfaces are rarely identified in documentation and

Photograph 11.5(a&b) Before and after. Traditional paving as a scarce resource - flagstones stolen from a street in Bristol

Photograph 11.6 Will these setts survive redevelopment of this site? Areas of 'paving at risk'? Canons Marsh, Bristol

184

therefore are subject to reduction by neglect and unsympathetic reinstatement. Some authorities such as Hove are compiling registers of streets with significant amounts of traditional paving in order that the Highways and Utilities are alerted to the significance of the surface.

b) Residential streets valued by residents but of insufficient 'special' character to merit Conservation Area designation. These streets are vulnerable and subject to sudden removal of surfaces by theft or replacement though a new maintenance regime (see figure 11.5). There is usually no record of these by the Planning departments and rarely by Highways. The emphasis needs to be in stocktaking and to assess local attitudes to the value placed on local floorscapes.

c) Areas likely to be totally overlooked or subject to redevelopment. Typically these may be station yards, cattle markets, waterfronts, factory areas, demolition sites, etc. Decisions need to be made as to the feasibility of either retaining paved areas in good condition and incorporating into a redevelopment scheme or taking up and storing those surfaces that are not likely to survive new highway or redevelopment proposals (see Figure 11.6). Storage of this stock might be justified to aid repaving or reinstatement in another area of the town.

The University of the West of England is, at the time of writing, undertaking audits of selected towns in the south west of England under the direction of the author. The aim of this project, part-funded by the Department of National Heritage and Marshall's Natural Stone is to a build-up of a database of paving traditions in the south west, the distribution of paving materials and, finally, to assess sources of supply and levels of risk as outlined above. The project involves survey work undertaken by local Civic Societies coordinated with the help of Civic Trust South West. Eventually it is envisaged that a national map of paving traditions will be produced.

The distribution of traditional paving materials

Preliminary indications from the Paving Study show that whilst local materials do give a certain character to various sub regions, imported materials have always played a part in the variety of floorscapes to be found. Imported materials were most often located in towns with close connections to a harbour or canal where materials could be easily and cheaply transported by sea. For example, Caithness stone can be found in London, Newcastle and Hove, and Cornish Granite is virtually ubiquitous, as is York stone. Interesting local sources are Lias in Somerset and Gloucestershire, Purbeck in the South and Pennant stones in South Wales and the Bristol area and pockets of glazed brick or red brick in the south

Photograph 11.7   Re-used granite kerbs and setts, Norwich. Colour,
texture and pattern stemming from the material

Photograph 11.8   York stone and other flagstones at a recycled paving
stone dealer's yard, Wiltshire

186

east and east. Cobbles (not to be confused with setts) were widespread but often replaced at a later date.

Recent expansion in the use of traditional materials

Quarrying for paving stone declined rapidly from the beginning of the 20th century until the 1980s where there has been a significant but still small scale expansion of the paving stone industry, chiefly with York stone, but with a number of lesser known quarries and stone types available. This expansion is due to the market being created by Conservation Area enhancement schemes and the proliferation of waterfront projects in the 1980s. A new-found emphasis on quality has resulted in the use of natural materials which weather well, retain their colour and are durable.

Is natural stone paving a sustainable source of surfacing for the public realm?

At first glance the answer to this question may seem to be 'no'; surely stone is a finite resource, the extraction of which tends to disfigure the landscape. However, if we consider the question again there do seem to be convincing arguments to the contrary. What are the alternatives to traditional paving units? Either tarmacadam or concrete based products reproducing the cosmetic effect of stone or brick. Whilst these products are undoubtedly cheaper when we take the bald price of supply and laying, other factors contribute to redressing the balance. Tarmacadam and reconstituted stone or concrete products tend to have a short life, requiring replacement over 15-20 years, whereas paving stone has a proven life of 150-200 years in the same streets it was laid. Moreover, even if stone is cracked, it can be trimmed and used elsewhere, and if worn it can be retooled if necessary (see Figures 11.7, 11.8). Finally, stone can be broken up to be used as hardcore or aggregate. Concrete products, being proprietary brands, tend to have limited 'shelf life', therefore replacement can be a problem in the longer term as designs and specifications change. Concrete will eventually break up into its constituent parts and any pigments used are likely to fade. A number of 'first generation' town centre pedestrianisation schemes laid about 20 years ago are being replaced either because they are proving difficult to maintain, are failing or are dated. Products based on crushed stone or bitumen usually require more energy consumption in their manufacture and laying; traditional flagstones and setts, on the other hand, are produced through fewer processes. The quarrying process itself is very efficient as all the stone is used; from large slabs to small, right down to slips, kerbs, setts and aggregate, depending on the stone type. Even the water used for cooling the cutting machinery is recycled.

The quarrying of natural paving materials

Whilst existing paving materials which would normally be lost through thoughtless removal and destruction, or areas over-surfaced could be identified, taken up and recycled, there will be a modest but increasing demand for the supply of newly quarried paving materials, if the call for their increased use finds a ready audience and market.

This leads us to the apparently vexed question: is this call requiring the extension or opening up of quarries? Let us examine the implications of this question. The vast majority of stone quarrying in Britain in the post war period has been for aggregate to supply an apparently insatiable demand for highway construction and building materials. 250 million tonnes per year are removed from hillsides in this capital intensive industry. Limestone and to a lesser extent sandstones and igneous rocks which give the variety of forms to our landscapes, are crushed to provide hardcore and aggregate for roadbuilding and the making of concrete or the ingredients for reconstructed stone blocks for the building industry. However, this demand has shown an appreciable dip since the early 1970s. For instance, in Somerset the seconnd leading county for quarrying in England the extraction in 1989 was 4 million tonnes from the high point of 6 million tonnes in 1973. Current government policy advocating reduced investment in major road building projects leads one to expect a continuation of this lower rate of extraction.

Virtually all of the County Minerals Policies are restrictive; the presumption being against the opening up of former or new quarries and the detailed requirements for screening, minimising nuisance to neighbouring development and the preparation of reinstatement plans. The intention seems to be to safeguard reserves by preventing the sterilisation of supply by inappropriate location of non-quarrying development, and in re-use of waste products whenever possible.

Stone for building and to a lesser extent that for paving hardly merit a mention in most minerals policies; Gloucestershire (for the Cotswolds) and Avon (for Bath stone) being exceptions. This is because the extraction rates for building stone are so low, for instance in Avon one of the three Bath stone quarries is producing 8,500 tonnes per year. A reasonable but unscientific extrapolation of this figure suggests that the extraction of stone for building and paving is likely to be less than 1% of the total being quarried. Not only are extraction rates low, the quarrying process for building and paving stone is less reliant on large scale machinery and does not require ancillary plant such as crushing equipment and bitumen binding. Obviously, nuisance from vehicles, dust generation and visual instrusion is a small fraction of that for the aggregate trade.

It is likely that any increase in the home supply of paving stone would be met from a combination of three approaches; using appropriate beds in existing quarries, reopening former quarries where feasible, and possibly opening up new sources where alternatives cannot be found. There are signs that this is happening. Near Yeovilton in Somerset a Lias quarry has been opened to provide a distinctive paving stone for domestic use and for street schemes in towns where this material was once widely used. In Surrey ironstone beds were exposed in an existing sand and gravel quarry. An enterprising paving contractor was able to extract this stone for use in paving an area in an enhancement scheme for a town where ironstone was characteristic, but where supplies were thought to be extinct or uneconomic for extraction. Many small quarries are experiencing an increasing demand; from the near-ideal smooth, precise, nonslip Caithness stone in north Scotland to the mellow Purbeck stone on the Dorset coast. Since 1990 Caithness stone quarries have expanded from one to five and now employ 17 people in an area of few choices of employment. This expansion has been responsive to demand for high quality paving in historic centres in Britain and mainland Europe.

It comes as a surprise therefore that the quarrying industry is a little slow in satisfying this increasing demand, and following the example of York stone suppliers in diversifying to create natural stone paving divisions. The massive reserves of excellent Pennant sandstone (from which the streets of south Wales, Bristol and Bath are paved) found in Gwent are being used solely for crushed stone; surely some can be used for paving? Similarly, Britain imports virtually all its granite for setts from Portugal; perhaps a proportion of the granite used for aggregate could be used for setts. As much of the cutting of granite for setts is mechanised then surely the difference in labour costs is not as great a factor as might be assumed.

Design of schemes using traditional paving materials

Traditional paving materials can be used in a less wasteful, more sustainable way if designers, specifiers and layers are more acquainted with the nature of the material and work with it, rather than imposing design and technical assumptions drawn from other fields. Schemes can prove unnecessarily costly if ill-considered decisions are taken and the advice of knowledgeable suppliers is ignored.

Experience is teaching us lessons in sustainable design:

> First: decide where to pave and where to use an aggregate finish. It is unwise to use paving slabs on a trafficked area as an unacceptably high number of breakages will occur and the surface will become discoloured. Most villages and smaller towns were never extensively paved and thus a surface dressing of a local aggregate or aggregate with a clear binding medium may be more appropriate. Setts are a good 'signalling' medium for shared pedestrian/vehicle surfaces, conveying a message of alertness for both users. It is wasteful and uncomfortable however to use setts for purely pedestrian areas.

> Second: avoid fussiness. Too many changes of material raise initial costs and the cost of reinstatement. A 'busy' effect is often produced which may have looked necessary on the expanse of a drawing board but when viewed with the foreshortening of the real life experience of perception in a crowded place is

entirely inappropriate. The natural variations in colour inherent in traditional materials are usually enough to create visual interest.

Third: consider the dimensioning of units. Designers trained to use manufactured units are conditioned to make all units a standard size to ensure an economical scheme. With natural stone almost the opposite is true. Due to the variable sizes of slabs extracted, the quarry operator will cut blocks to a range of sizes, say 2 or 3 widths and a larger range of lengths. The effect of this variation will give a pleasant rhythm to a street layout and further subtle variety to the restrained choice of material. The maximum size of slab should be related to the ease of handling and transportation. Some designers have been known to specify slabs of such a size they are physically impossible or too expensive to handle and are of course susceptible to cracking if subjected to point loads where the sub-base might be uneven.

Fourth: order the stone in sufficient time. Natural stone is rarely an 'off the shelf' product, therefore some time is required for cutting and preparation. Last minute orders may thus be more costly.

Fifth: insist on skilled workforce for laying and reinstatement. The laying of paving is a skilled job both in techniques and having a good eye for setting out and cutting slabs. A scheme can prove a success or failure at this stage. Smooth surfaces and close jointing can be achieved to a standard which is acceptable to access groups and pram pushers. The scheme can then be lost by poor reinstatement with little or no trained supervision. The New Roads & Streetworks Act 1991 goes some way in requiring a reasonable standard of reinstatement.

Sixth: ensure an effective maintenance and cleaning regime is in place. This is the unglamorous but essential ingredient of any sustainable design system.

Conclusion

The emphasis on attaining quality and sustainability in the built environment is likely to mean that traditional paving materials will be used on an increasing scale in the public realm. However tarmacadam and concrete will retain their supremacy where cost and vehicular considerations will predominate. Nevertheless, wherever a sense of local distinctiveness is seen to need reinforcement through reflecting the varied geology of Britain then traditional paving materials will have a part to play. Their innate sense of permanence, texture and colour has an undeniable value. Moreover, in fostering traditional materials opportunities open up for small scale enterprise and employment in rural areas, whenever the quarrying industry wishes to develop this new market.

References

Department of the Environment, URBED (1994), *Vital & Viable Town Centres*, HMSO: London.

Department of the Environment (1994), *PPG 6 Town Centres and Retail Development*, HMSO: London.

Davies, P. (1991), 'Improvements in Historic Areas'. *Conservation Bulletin 15*, English Heritage: London.

English Heritage (1993), *Street Improvements in Historic Areas*, English Heritage: London.

English Historic Towns Forum (1994), *Traffic in Historic Town Centres*, English Historic Towns Forum: Bath.

Guise, R. and Green, N. (eds) (1994), *Traditional Paving Design*. Conference Proceedings, University of the West of England and Somerset County Council: Bristol.

Guise, R. (1994), 'The Value of Traditional Paving in the Street Scene' *Streets Ahead Conference Proceedings*, University of the West of England: Bristol.